# In Search of a Voice:
# Karaoke and the Construction
# of Identity in Chinese America

**Everyday Communication: Case Studies of Behavior in Context**
*Wendy Leeds-Hurwitz & Stuart J. Sigman, Series Editors*

*Smooth Talkers: The Linguistic Performance of Auctioneers and Sportscasters*
  Koenraad Kuiper

*In Search of a Voice: Karaoke and the Construction of Identity in Chinese America*
  Casey Man Kong Lum

*Confrontation Talk: Arguments, Asymmetries, and Power on Talk Radio*
  Ian Hutchby

# In Search of a Voice: Karaoke and the Construction of Identity in Chinese America

**Casey Man Kong Lum**
*Adelphi University*

**LEA**  LAWRENCE ERLBAUM ASSOCIATES, PUBLISHERS
1996  Mahwah, New Jersey

Lawrence Erlbaum Associates, Inc., Publishers
10 Industrial Avenue
Mahwah, New Jersey  07430

Cover design by Mairav Salomon-Dekel

**Library of Congress Cataloging-in-Publication Data**

Lum, Casey Man Kong
        In search of a voice : karaoke and the construction of
    identity in Chinese America / Casey Man Kong Lum.
        p.  cm.
        Includes bibliographical references and index.
        ISBN   0-8058-1911-8   (alk.   paper).   —   ISBN
    0-8058-1912-6 (pbk. : alk. paper)
        1.  Chinese Americans—Music.   2.  Karaoke—Social
    aspects—United States. 3. Chinese Americans—Social life
    and customs. I.  Title.
    ML3560.C5L8  1996
    306.4'84—dc20                                      95-25506
                                                          CIP

Books published by Lawrence Erlbaum Associates are printed
on acid-free paper, and their bindings are chosen for strength
and durability.

Printed in the United States of America
10  9  8  7  6  5  4  3  2  1

*In memory of my beloved father, Chi Kau Wong,*
*whose voice I can no longer remember*

# Contents

# Foreword

If Dr. Lum's book were only about karaoke and its meaning to Chinese Americans, it would be well worth reading. For then, it would be a book about something new and strange. But the book is much more than that, and has an importance that goes beyond the study of one cultural artifact and one group of people.

It is, first of all, an example of a method of gaining insight into how people integrate a new medium into their ways of living. Scholars will find here a refreshing approach to inquiry; a method that elevates and enriches the study of media; a graceful blend of the techniques used by anthropologists, sociologists, and psychologists.

The book is also about the striving for identity which, in a multicultural society, is always a necessity. Using Dr. Lum's analysis as a starting point, readers will have no difficulty in understanding why and how other groups of people use new media to give strength and uniqueness to their sense of themselves. This means that the book is also about America and about its immigrant subcultures. It is about how immigrants struggle to become Americans while holding onto traditions that originated in far away places.

Dr. Lum knows all about these things and tells us what he knows with clarity, affection, and charm.

*Neil Postman*

# Editors' Preface

This second volume in the Everyday Communication series continues our interest in the contextualization of symbolic processes. The series is devoted to the publication of case studies concerning patterns of human communication behavior placed within relevant cultural and social contexts. Casey Lum's *In Search of a Voice: Karaoke and the Construction of Identity in Chinese America* contributes to this editorial mission, and then some.

Lum's book is the result of ethnographic fieldwork among foreign-born Chinese Americans living in the New York–New Jersey metropolitan area. Lum conducted participant observation and informant interviewing in order to gauge the acceptance and meaning of karaoke technology for this immigrant group. The book provides a rich overview of the ways in which a new communication technology is integrated into a community's existing social and cultural experiences, at the same time facilitating changes among those who adopt it. The book is in the tradition of Harold Innis, Marshall McLuhan, and Neil Postman in one respect, and the tradition of Clifford Geertz and Erving Goffman in another. The McLuhanesque angle arises from Lum's consideration of the "biases" inherent in this new technology. The book demonstrates that the technology itself places demands on people's literacy skills, their vocal abilities, and the kinds of physical spaces in which the technology is used. The Geertzian angle arises from Lum's demonstration that technology is not completely deterministic with regard to its integration into people's lives. Different communities may assign contrasting meaning and significance to a symbolic medium; may employ a communication technology in ways that express each community's history, cultural traditions, longings, and so on; and may give rise to a new "voice," that is, new forms of cultural expression.

The two strands of analysis come together through Lum's contextualization of his informants' karaoke activities. Simply put, Chinese America is not a homogeneous community or a univocal experience. From the available data, *In Search of a Voice* teases out three component communities: successful professionals who engage in karaoke occasions to enhance their public reputations and social standing, and who organize and prepare for their karaoke events in much the same ways they do their careers; moderately prosperous working- and middle-class members for whom karaoke is a means to revitalize an older form of operatic performance; and transient immigrants who have access to karaoke equipment only in public venues like restaurants and who engage with this as part of a psychological escape from their difficult working and living conditions. The analysis shows that there are socio-economic and ethnic (e.g., Cantonese, Malaysian, Taiwanese) factors that explain membership in one of these three communities and that within the various communities there are gender distinctions as well. As mentioned, the analysis also shows those areas of divergence in the uses of and meanings assigned to karaoke by the three communities, and those areas of convergence, where the karaoke technology exerts itself on the various community members.

In sum, *In Search of a Voice* enables us to consider the diverse karaoke contexts in which performers and audience members interact with each other and with the technology; it also permits us to contextualize those karaoke scenes in terms of the socioeconomic and ethnic communities in which the performers and audience members live.

*Wendy Leeds-Hurwitz*
*Stuart J. Sigman*

# Acknowledgments

I have discovered that writing a book is as humbling an experience as it is a wonderful educational opportunity. Writing this book has been a humbling experience because, in the process of thinking and writing, I have come to realize that I know so little about everything I originally thought I knew. It has been a wonderful educational opportunity because many scholars, authors, friends, and, especially, the many people I met and studied in the field sites tolerated my ignorance and taught me what I should have known.

First and foremost, for that reason, I am most grateful to Wendy Leeds-Hurwitz and Stuart J. Sigman for their endearing trust and friendship. From my first e-mail presentation in 1993 of the book idea to the final draft of the manuscript in 1995, Wendy and Stuart have never failed to be patient, thoughtful, and supportive in helping me develop, write, and refine the project. It has been my extreme good fortune to work with and learn from them.

My heartfelt appreciation also goes to Johan Fornäs (Media/Musicology, Stockholm University), Deborah Wong (Music, University of Pennsylvania), K. Scott Wong (History, Williams College), and Judy Yung (American Studies, University of California, Santa Cruz). Their very insightful reading and constructive criticism of an earlier draft of the entire manuscript helped me confront many conceptual and, on some occasions, historical inconsistencies. Deborah Wong, in particular, has continued to contribute to my initial education in ethnomusicology.

I would also like to thank Bell Yung (Music, University of Pittsburgh), whose scholarship in Chinese music and, particularly, Cantonese opera, assisted me enormously in writing and revising what is chapter 3. He also put me in touch with the fields of oral performance and folklore studies. I am in debt to Toru Mitsui (Music, Kanazawa University, Japan) for commenting on an earlier draft of chapter 1 and teaching me many things about Japanese karaoke. My gratitude also goes to Merry White (Sociology, Boston University and Edwin O. Reischauer Institute of Japanese Studies, Harvard University), who helped me explain certain social functions of karaoke in Japanese society.

I am most thankful to Thom Gencarelli (Broadcasting, Montclair State University), a wonderful friend and intellectual companion since my days at New York University in the late 1980s, who has patiently served as a "sounding board" for many of the ideas I address in this book. Similarly, his study of heavy metal music as communication (Gencarelli, 1993) has been a source of inspiration.

Many people have contributed to my education, particularly in culture and technology. Peter Haratonik (Communication, Hofstra University) has never failed to guide me, first as my teacher in the Media Studies Program at the New School for Social Research in the early 1980s and later as my mentor when I became a practitioner in the discipline. My teachers at New York University's Media Ecology Program, Neil Postman, Terence Moran, Christine Nystrom, and Henry Perkinson, taught me the joy of thinking, writing, and teaching about ideas and the importance of learning by always taking people's criticism seriously.

Although I have benefited from all of these people in writing this book, both directly and indirectly, any error remaining is entirely mine. It must also be noted that my acknowledgment of those individuals who have read and commented on earlier drafts of this study does not necessarily imply their agreement with the opinions and interpretations I express in this book.

I don't think I can ever sufficiently thank my mother, Siu Ling Lau, for without her life-long sacrifice and nurture, I would not have gone this far.

Above all, I would like to dedicate this book to my wife, Jenny Chia Chen Liu, whose love and friendship have been a source of great joy in good times and enormous strength through rainy days; and to our two boys, Xuanmin and Haumin, whose very presence alone is enough to make our lives all the more worthwhile.

*Casey Man Kong Lum*

# 1

# Understanding Karaoke as Communication

The word *karaoke* is a hybrid term consisting of two components: *kara,* meaning empty, and *oke,* an abbreviation of *okesutora,* an adopted foreign word in the Japanese vocabulary meaning "orchestra." Taking the separate elements together, karaoke means "orchestra minus one [the lead vocal]," which refers to prerecorded musical accompaniments designed for amateur singing.[1] The word also denotes either a place (such as a bar or a nightclub with karaoke entertainment) or a machine that allows users to sing with prerecorded musical accompaniments.

To the novice, singing karaoke, especially before a group of strangers, can be a nerve-wracking experience. I can vividly remember how I felt the first time I attended a karaoke event. Not unlike many first-timers, I went through a series of complex yet memorable emotions during that first karaoke experience: the excitement, the anticipation, the anxiety, the excuses, the self-doubt, the urge to show off, and so forth. My first karaoke encounter took place in the summer of 1993 at a friend's barbecue party on Long Island. No one mentioned to me beforehand that karaoke was on the agenda. Perhaps it was not planned ahead of time. But when the grill in the backyard was slowly cooling off, our hosts Richard and Diane suggested that the seven or eight of us sing karaoke in the large living room. The thought that I might have to sing before a group of people, most of whom I had met only a few hours before, caused anticipation as well as anxiety. It had never occurred to me that I was even remotely close to being musically competent enough to sing in public.

[1]The word karaoke has been translated literally as "empty orchestra" (e.g., see Feiler, 1991, p. 51; Shelley, 1993, p. 159). But according to Toru Mitsui, in the original Japanese conception of karaoke, "kara" carries the connotation of "without [the voice]" instead of the literal meaning of "empty" (personal communication, April 10, 1995). Mitsui has written on the history of karaoke in Japan and, at this writing, is the president of the International Association for the Study of Popular Music. Yoshio Tanaka (1990) similarly referred to karaoke as sound tracks minus the lead vocal.

Richard, an entrepreneur in his late 30s who immigrated to the United States early in the 1980s, took only a few moments to set up his karaoke system. Before long, he was singing a song by the Beatles in front of the rest of the group. To be exact, it was not actually a Beatles recording, but a laserdisc video that reproduced the accompaniment of a Beatles song featuring four impersonators. I felt the video was kind of ridiculous and the impersonators looked and acted silly. But my mind was so overwhelmed by the anticipation that the hosts might ask me to sing that I cannot even remember which Beatles song it was.

Only three from the party were active in singing that evening. The rest, including me, spent most of the time watching and, perhaps, worrying. But that did not mean that we were left alone. The hosts passed the wireless microphone to us every so often—between songs, or even between two verses—but the rest of us avoided it as if it would burn us. I offered all kinds of excuses, both publicly and in my own mind, to stay away from the fearsome-looking microphone. "I'm still digesting my food," I found myself saying to Richard at one point. In my weakest moment of the evening, I even gave myself the shameless excuse of "I'm doing research here" for not joining in the singing.

Halfway through the evening, however, I began to notice a gradual change in my reaction to the event, particularly after the hosts sang a few songs that were familiar to me—those that I often heard over the radio or hummed in the shower. Although the fear of making a fool of myself still stood between me and the microphone, the intensity of my hesitation subsided. Meanwhile, Richard and Diane were becoming indifferent to the few of us who were not singing. They did not ask us to sing as often as before. I began to develop a sense of unease, feeling a bit out of place. "I hope they are not upset with me," I thought.

My "moment" finally came when Paul McCartney's "Hey Jude" was finishing with those long "la . . . la . . . la . . . la la la la, la la la la, hey Jude" phrases. The hosts were crooning along and I, almost imperceptibly, eased into the chorus. "La . . . la . . . la . . . la la la la . . . " Feeling no objection from the hosts and seeing no apparent unusual reaction from the others, especially my wife, I began to sing louder and louder. ". . . La la la la . . . hey Jude."

A few numbers later, I picked Don McLean's "Vincent" for my solo debut—a song that I have always loved to listen to and hum. I sang it all by myself, before all those people, but it took me less than a minute to realize that I really could not sing the song. I was off by a couple of keys. I ran out of breath numerous times. I tended to sing ahead of the lyrics, or, at times, I was chasing after them. By the middle of the song, I began to feel that the song was much longer than I thought.

In the car on our way home, I busily wondered whether everyone at the party had discovered how badly I had sung. But, almost miraculously, my wife told me how very surprised she was that I could sing so well. "So well?!" I thought. I was puzzled by my wife's compliment because I knew she actually meant what she said. Nonetheless, I began to feel better about my singing.

For several days afterward, I could not help but think about the various emotions I had experienced that evening: from the anxiety to the longing to be part of the group, and from the positive approval of an otherwise mediocre performance to the willful acceptance of such a compliment. Also, I thought about how casual and invisible karaoke as a form of entertainment and popular culture had already become to Richard and Diane, as well as to the millions of people like them in various parts of Asia, in overseas Asian immigrant communities, and, increasingly, around the world. I wanted to know more.

I begin this book with my first karaoke experience not only because it was memorable but, more importantly, because it reflects the typical responses that people have when they first encounter karaoke. Although many people share these initial emotional responses, the significance they eventually generate through, or attach to, their karaoke experience may differ from one social context to another. In fact, it is the purpose of this book to examine how karaoke may be engaged in in a great variety of ways, and how varying social meanings can be constructed through the use of karaoke in different everyday contexts.

This book is an ethnography of how karaoke is used in the expression, maintenance, and (re)construction of social identity as part of the Chinese American experience. It explores the social and theoretical implications of interaction between the media audience and karaoke as both an electronic communication technology and a cultural practice. As such, the book has its theoretical foundations resting on a nexus of three areas of analysis: namely, cultural adaptation of communication technology, audience interaction with electronic media, and the role of media in the evolution of the Chinese diaspora in the United States.

To construct an analytical framework for our discussion, I offer three preliminary theoretical assumptions. First, karaoke events can be studied as cultural practices through an analysis of the interaction among the various human, circumstantial, material, and symbolic elements that they are comprised of. Second, because karaoke events are by nature social, participation in a karaoke event has intended and unintended social ramifications for the participants that can be studied by analyzing the meanings the participants derive from, or attach to, their karaoke experience. Third, the meanings that people attach to their karaoke experience can be studied by analyzing how they approach their participation in karaoke events. Because karaoke events exist in everyday social contexts, participants' interpretation of their karaoke experiences must be understood in the context of their general social experience and everyday life.

In the rest of this chapter, I explain in theoretical terms how karaoke can be analyzed as a technology and as a cultural practice. Moreover, I look at the dramaturgical nature of karaoke and the role of people in the construction and maintenance of their identity in the social contexts of karaoke. To place the theoretical discussion and the ensuing case studies in concrete historical and social contexts, chapter 2 examines how karaoke should and can be viewed as part of the general media experience in the Chinese American diaspora.

Using the theoretical, historical, and sociological framework constructed in this and the next chapters as my guide, chapters 3, 4, and 5 present and analyze the divergent karaoke experiences of three interpretive communities of first-generation Chinese American immigrants. These include people in the Hong Kong Cantonese, Taiwanese, and Malaysian Chinese immigrant communities in the New York and New Jersey greater metropolitan area. Chapter 6 offers a final analysis and synthesis of the findings from this study. Methodological notes are presented in the Appendix.

## KARAOKE: TECHNOLOGY AND CULTURAL PRACTICES

A communication technology is the material embodiment of human ideas for solving certain pre-existing, real, or perceived problems relating to information or human interaction. Pre-existing human conditions, therefore, play a vital role in the conception, development, and adoption (or rejection) of a communication technology. The technology of writing, for example, was conceived partially as a means to preserve and manipulate information in a way that human memory alone was incapable of doing (Havelock, 1976; Ong, 1982). In early Modern Europe, the metal movable type printing press was invented to reproduce information on a large scale, freeing scribes from the tedious job of manual copying, a process that frequently introduced errors (Eisenstein, 1979).

Of course, communication technology is more than just a problem solver. Whereas a new technology resolves some pre-existing communication problem, it simultaneously introduces changes into the social ecology. It can help define or redefine how people relate among themselves. With writing, people no longer have to rely on solely oral, face-to-face, and spontaneous communications to interact with each other. During its inception, writing was in fact perceived as a serious challenge to the art and culture of oral discourse and the human dialectic that Socrates so endeared and vigorously defended (see the *Phaedrus*). The printing press further intensified the separation or alienation between the speakers and writers and their audiences while helping to give rise to an ever-expanding reading public. By its very nature, as

Elizabeth L. Eisenstein (1983) suggested, "a reading public was ، more dispersed; it was also more atomistic and individualistic ‿ا a hearing one" (p. 94). At another level, the new class of writers and printers in early Modern Europe helped democratize information and knowledge from centuries of control by the monastic, scribal elites (Eisenstein, 1979), thus reconfiguring the power relations between the producers and consumers of information.

There is another kind of power relations embedded in technology: Socially constructed gender roles are implicated in the conception, development, and use of communication technology. Technology, according to Lana Rakow (1988), "is a site where social practices are embedded and express and extend the construction of two asymmetrical genders" (p. 56). This conception suggests that the gender relations embedded in technology are symptomatic of how people of the two genders interplay and negotiate the construction, maintenance, and/or transformation of their respective place in the social order. According to this view, technology is not gender neutral, particularly when gender relations play a role in determining people's access to or use of technology. For example, Shaun Moores (1993) noted that, in 1920s Britain, the father in the family was often the monopolizing user of early wireless when the radio set in the household had only one audio output through a headphone. David Morley (1986) documented how men in his study dominated the use of the television remote control device; that is, commanded the choice of programs during family viewing.

In reviewing these gendered uses of the wireless headphones and the remote control devices in their respective time frames and social spaces, Moores (1993) suggested the following: "In both instances, a newly arrived piece of technological hardware becomes a symbolic site of (principally gendered) frictions within the family context" (p. 80).

But the fact that a new communication technology can help to introduce and facilitate changes or buttress certain pre-existing social norms does not mean that such changes or affirmations will inevitably or uniformly occur in other societies where the same technology is also adopted. In his fascinating study of technology and social change in Medieval Europe, Lynn White, Jr. (1962) observed:

> As our understanding of the history of technology increases, it becomes clear that a new device merely opens a door; it does not compel one to enter. The acceptance or rejection of an invention, or the extent to which its implications are realized if it is accepted, depends quite as much upon the condition of a society, and upon the imagination of its leaders, as upon the technological item itself. (p. 28)[2]

[2]In making the previous observation, White (1962) specifically referred to how Charles Martel, the Frankish military leader in the eighth century, adopted the stirrup to facilitate a fighting technique called mounted shock combat. Before it, horses were typically used to

A technology can be adopted in ways as diverse as the needs and aspirations of the people in the adopting societies. Depending on the specific contexts, different social uses of a technology may yield different or even unforeseen outcomes. Therefore, to understand the cultural adaptation of technology, it is not enough to know what the technology can do. It is imperative to know how and why the technology is used in its particular social contexts of adaptation.[3] It is also important to look at how the uses interplay with other forces in society, such as economic distributions and gender arrangements that determine people's access to technology.

As I examine in more detail, the cultural practice of amateur participatory singing in Japan (and elsewhere) predated the physical apparatus used in the formulation of karaoke technology. The basic audio, video, and laser recording, storage, and retrieval technologies used in karaoke were originally invented in the West (Straubhaar & LaRose, 1996) and subsequently diffused to other parts of the world. Although these technologies were gradually adopted around the world, it was in the social and cultural context of post-World War II Japan where they were reconfigured into a new, hybrid technology form in the service of a pre-existing cultural practice of communal singing. Before I examine the original social contexts for the emergence of karaoke, however, I clarify further the notion of karaoke singing as a cultural practice.

**Karaoke as a Cultural Practice**

In conceiving karaoke singing as a cultural practice, I use the word *culture* in much the same way as Clifford Geertz's (1973) vivid concep-

---

transport warriors to the battlefields, where they would dismount and engage in combat on foot. However, not only did the stirrup allow a warrior to do combat on horseback, it allowed the mounted warrior to deliver a brutal blow with his lance "with the combined weight of himself and his charging stallion" (White, 1962, p. 2) and doing so without the customary fear and frequent consequence of falling off his horse. Unlike the Franks, the Anglo-Saxons used the stirrup but did not realize its full military potential, a fact that they regretted later. As the most mobile and lethal fighting machines on horseback, the stirruped Franks took over the lands once controlled by the Church and distributed them to vassals and eventually became the masters of Europe and changed the face of feudalism in the Middle Ages.

[3]Neil Postman (1985) articulated this point by making a distinction between technology and medium:

We might say that a technology is to a medium as the brain is to the mind. Like the brain, a technology is a physical apparatus. Like the mind, a medium is a use to which a physical apparatus is put. A technology becomes a medium as it employs a particular symbolic code, as it finds its place in a particular social setting, as it insinuates itself into economic and political contexts. A technology, in other words, is merely a machine. A medium is the social and intellectual environment a machine creates. (p. 84) tualization: "Believing, with Max Weber, that man is an animal suspended in webs of significance he himself has spun, I take culture to be those webs, and the analysis of it to be therefore not an experimental science in search of law but an interpretive one in search of meaning" (p. 5). There is an intimate relationship between this interpretive anthropological conception of culture and the ritual view of communication, characterized by James W. Carey (1988) as "a symbolic process whereby reality is produced, maintained, repaired, and transformed" (p. 23). To study communication from this perspective, as Carey pointed out, "is to examine the actual social process wherein significant symbolic forms are created, apprehended, and used" (p. 30). Communication is an ongoing, sense-making experience whereby people, by using shared symbols, negotiate and determine among themselves the legitimate, the significant, or the sensible; that is, their social reality, the essence of their culture. Therefore, I take culture to mean the ways that people interact through material, symbolic, and/or institutional means; and the meanings, values, or significance they derive from or attach to such interactions. Culture manifests, perpetuates, and transforms itself through and in communication.

Reflecting on this conception of culture and communication, we can begin to conceptualize culture at the systemic level; that is, at the level of definable, individual systems. Raymond Williams (1965) suggested that "a culture" is

> a particular way of life which expresses certain meanings and values not only in art and learning, but also in institutions and ordinary behaviour. The analysis of culture, from such a definition, is the clarification of the meanings and values implicit and explicit in a particular way of life, a particular culture. (cited in Hebdige, 1979, p. 6)

To study a particular culture or cultural system, therefore, is to study the symbiosis among the human, material, symbolic, and institutional elements in society in the articulation of a particular way of life. We can begin to see how karaoke singing can be analyzed as a cultural practice. Karaoke embodies a process of human interactions and practices whereby certain values, meanings, or social realities are created, maintained, and transformed as part of a culture—a particular way of life. By extension, different ways to engage karaoke represent the articulations of different ways of life. To study Chinese American immigrant karaoke, therefore, is to study how karaoke is engaged in as an everyday practice in the construction, articulation, and interpretation of those meanings that are part of the Chinese American immigrant experience. This leads to the following question: What cultural practice does karaoke embody? To address this question, I examine in the next section the social origins of karaoke in Japan.

## Social Origins of Karaoke

Karaoke as a communication technology came into being under a most appropriate set of social conditions. Before mass-produced karaoke sets came along, bar patrons singing to the tunes of professional musicians had long been a tradition in Kobe, a thriving seaport metropolis in Western Japan. Overlooking Osaka Bay, Kobe owes part of its glamour to its lively musical nightlife. The proliferation of cassette tape recorders also facilitated an interest in singing among many in Japan, chiefly among men in their 40s and 50s (Ogawa, 1990). The late 1960s and early 1970s saw a revival of *enka* (traditional Japanese songs of unrequited love) among these middle-aged men, who felt out of place with the dominating, Western-tinged popular music that was then catering to the young in Japan (T. Mitsui, personal communication, April 10, 1995). But there were efforts to reduce the cost of providing live music in drinking or entertainment establishments, where many middle-aged *enka* devotees drank and socialized after work. Experiments were attempted with several sound media, such as reel-to-reel tapes and jukeboxes.

The prototype of commercial karaoke sets did not appear until 1972. At the time, entrepreneur and musician Daisuke Inoue and his colleagues in Kobe introduced eight-track cartridges of their own musical performances without any vocal elements (Mitsui, 1991). One such cartridge contained four accompaniments of two tracks each. Technically, the eight-track loop cartridge gives its users easy access to the four accompaniments: The loop goes back to the beginning as any one of the accompaniments comes to an end. Special machines were built for these tapes. Each karaoke set was built with integrated microphone inputs, an echo mechanism, and a coin slot. What was particularly unique about Inoue's tapes and the machine, as Mitsui pointed out, was that they were the first commercial accompaniment tapes and karaoke systems meant for amateur singers.

In short, the various experiments to reduce the costs of providing live music at drinking and entertainment establishments where *enka* reigned set up the immediate context for the conceptual and technological development of karaoke in Japan. Because *enka* was the most popular musical genre at the drinking or entertainment establishments where commercially available karaoke evolved, it represented the majority of the karaoke repertoire in its first decade in existence (T. Mitsui, personal communication, April 10, 1995).

Meanwhile, the Japanese love of singing helped serve as a fertile ground for the germination and spread of karaoke to other segments in Japan's population and for the development of musical genres other than *enka*. As Boye De Mente (1989) observed:

For centuries, the Japanese have been raised on lullabies and folk songs and have learned how to sing as a natural part of growing up. Everybody is expected to join in the singing of festivals, and, at parties and other kinds of gatherings, it is customary for individuals to take turns singing. (p. 158)

Because social amateur singing was a pre-existing cultural practice in Japan, what karaoke as a technology did for that aspect of Japanese culture was make musical accompaniments more readily available to people when they wanted to sing. Therefore, karaoke as a technology is the material embodiment of a set of pre-existing cultural practices, arrangements for human interaction in everyday life—or what Erving Goffman (1983) called the interaction order. Karaoke encapsulates a "web of significance," an interaction structure that, given its social and cultural roots, fosters the building and maintenance of group membership or community through participatory singing. This partially helps explain why karaoke singing has become a popular cultural form among people of all ages in Japan (Ban, 1991; Nunziata, 1990; Ogawa, 1993b; White, 1993).[4] Similarly, Deborah Wong (1994) suggested that the love of amateur singing in certain parts of Asia helps explain why karaoke has been popular in those regions (see also "Karaoke is," 1992).

The first U. S. karaoke bars appeared in 1983, catering to a mostly "Asian clientele" (Zimmerman, 1991, p. 108), which, as Mitsui suggested (personal communication, April 10, 1995), might have been predominantly Japanese business people working in the United States and Japanese Americans. Toward the end of the 1980s, bars catering to a more general American clientele, along with certain commercial publicists, started to use karaoke as a promotional tool (Armstrong, 1992).[5] Whereas the general population in the United States is still warming

---

[4]Merry White (personal communication, October 12, 1993), a Boston University sociologist and a research fellow at Harvard University's Edwin O. Reischauer Institute of Japanese Studies, added yet another interesting explanation for why karaoke has become a popular form of entertainment in Japan. She suggested the following:

> Japanese don't invite people home. A karaoke bar or club is a home from home. It's always important that there is a place where one can entertain friends. Home is not a place to entertain guests, especially if they are not one's own family. It's been said that Japanese don't invite friends over because houses in Japan are small. But that's not really it. It is about a sense of a home, a place that is inviolable. It is a private space where one can indulge in total freedom without having to put on special masks.

Karaoke offers the Japanese an important alternative space for maintaining social relations with people from outside the family.

[5]Around the same time, the consumer electronics manufacturer Pioneer marketed the world's first laserdisc karaoke systems for the consumer market (Ogawa, 1993a).

up to the idea of singing karaoke in bars, certain definable cultural practices that center around karaoke have already emerged among many in Chinese America.[6] Much like their cousins in Asia, where karaoke is widely popular, many Chinese Americans from diverse social, economic, and ethnic backgrounds engage in a great variety of karaoke activities: self-entertainment, social gatherings, performance, or festive events, and so forth. Social networks are formed around a common interest in karaoke. Indeed, not only has karaoke become a popular form of entertainment for many Chinese Americans, some have adopted karaoke as a cultural practice central to their social existence.

However, how can we conceptualize karaoke as a cultural practice? How is the web of karaoke constructed as a communal event or cultural experience? What does the social or symbolic structure of karaoke look like? To address these questions, the next section analyzes the "dramaturgical web of karaoke."

## THE DRAMATURGICAL WEB OF KARAOKE

Because karaoke embodies human interactions in specific social contexts, I use Goffman's (1959) dramaturgical metaphor to conceptualize the web of karaoke.[7] It is important to note, however, that Goffman's focus of analysis was on "social establishments as relatively closed systems" (p. 239). The extent to which we can view karaoke as a closed or open system has yet to be determined. Thus, in this section, I use the dramaturgical metaphor only as an initial analytical framework to conceptualize the karaoke web as a definable social environment wherein people play various roles in an ongoing process of interaction and impression management. In reference to the conception of karaoke as a cultural practice, I first look at the organizational, material, and symbolic components that help construct the dramaturgical site of the karaoke scene.

---

[6]Karaoke is also popular in many other Asian American communities. For example, Wong (1994) studied the karaoke experience of certain Vietnamese Americans in the Los Angeles area and Robert Drew's (1994) dissertation touched on certain aspects of Japanese-American karaoke bars in and around the Philadelphia area. But because Asian America is a complex sociopolitical space, and because karaoke as a serious scholarly subject is a relatively uncharted area, I delimit my discussion to only certain social and cultural aspects of the Chinese American karaoke experience.

[7]Drew's (1994) analysis of what he called the performance frame of karaoke in the context of mainstream U.S. bars in Philadelphia also partially adopts Goffman's (1959) dramaturgical metaphor. However, we developed our respective studies independent of each other, and have generated different uses of Goffman's work.

## The Karaoke Scene

A karaoke scene is an event where karaoke singing is the defining activity that facilitates interaction among the participants. It is normally composed of a number of episodes; that is, smaller units of interaction. As with any social event, every karaoke scene is set in a specific social occasion and time. The specific social occasion in which a karaoke scene occurs necessarily gives direction to what happens there, in much the same way that a script helps to lay out the plot of a movie or a play. The occasion can be a birthday party, a formal evening gala, a business dinner, a weekly gathering among friends, everyday entertainment at home, or the like. Embedded in each of these occasions are certain explicit and implicit expectations of the roles that participants play to facilitate the general progress of the scene. At a certain level, the scripts for the scene resemble what A. E. Scheflen (1964, 1965, 1979) called *programs;* that is, "patterns of behavior" (1979, p. 10) or "traditional formats or templates, learned and used by each member of a culture, that determine behavior" (1964, p. 317).

Every karaoke scene is located in a *setting,* the physical context where the scene's human interaction takes place. The physical layout and decor of the environment of the karaoke event also provide symbolic meanings. Similarly, props such as karaoke equipment and costumes such as the clothing and accessories that participants wear support the progress of the scene and give a symbolic reference to the nature of the occasion. Specifically, the setting, props, and costumes connote the participants' style, taste, social class, or any combination of these elements.

## Areas of Actions

What distinguishes karaoke scenes from most other social scenes are the two distinct areas of action in what Goffman (1959) referred to as the "front region" (p. 107), and, in particular, how participants move between these two areas and the dramaturgical implication of this movement.[8] I refer to the *stage area* as the space where the karaoke system, the most significant and defining equipment of any karaoke scene, is located and utilized and where the formal singing of karaoke takes place. The physical layout of the stage area varies from one scene to another, ranging from the entertainment center of someone's living room to a platform in an expensive karaoke nightclub or a temporary space created for Karaoke Night at a bar.

---

[8]Goffman (1959) distinguished the front region from the back region. My analysis here only considers two aspects of the front region—the stage area and the audience area; it also reveals a permeability of the boundary between stage and audience areas not previously studied by Goffman. The role of rehearsal and training—backstage behavior—is discussed in later chapters.

Facing the stage area is what I consider the *audience area,* the space wherein the rest of the participants witness the karaoke performance as an audience. Depending on the social context or the setup of the stage area, the physical layout of the audience area also varies from one scene to another. In general, sitting arrangements for the audience are usually provided for and may include such variations as sofas in someone's living room, dining tables and chairs at a nightclub or restaurant, or stools at a bar.

It is important to note that the stage area and the audience area are not always distinguishable from one another in every karaoke setting. In many Japanese-style entertainment establishments, in both Japan itself and overseas Japanese communities, for example, long microphone cables or cordless microphones allow the singing customers to perform without leaving their table. The line between the stage area and the audience area in a karaoke box is also blurred. A karaoke box is a small rental room designed specifically for karaoke singing. In it, the karaoke system is placed at one end of the room opposite a sitting area, where the performer and the audience both congregate.

### The Dual Role of Karaoke Participants

The uniqueness of this spatial arrangement (stage area vs. audience area) in the karaoke front region lies in the fact that it signifies two different roles for the participants. In most social settings, participants need to play only one role in the front region, for example, as diners eating lunch in a restaurant or as audience members watching a play in a theater. In the front region of a karaoke scene, however, there is always a chance that a participant will travel between the two areas, playing two different roles. All karaoke participants are, by implication of their being present at the scene, potential performers as well as audience members. Customarily, performers in any karaoke scene come from the audience. As Hiroshi Ogawa (1993a) put it, this lack of clear-cut separation between audience and performer has implications for how all the participants are perceived:

> Karaoke encloses a "karaoke space" with its music wall. People there are thought to be friends. And a person singing in the presence of the others in spite of shyness is thought to be trusted. Both sharing a "karaoke space" and singing in the presence of the others reinforce group consciousness. (p. 2)

The participants in a karaoke event are there both to entertain and be entertained by others. This mutual entertainment encourages a certain degree of bonding among participants in the scene, for, as Ogawa implied, people in the karaoke scene regard each other as friends.

However, I can analyze how this bonding is maintained from a slightly different perspective. Because there is a customary expectation that audience members will take a turn singing sooner or later during the course of the event, no karaoke participant risks denigrating the performance of others, at least not in public view or in the front region. Knowing they may later perform in the stage area and be judged by those re-entering the audience area, karaoke participants minimally criticize the performances before them. Thus the reciprocity inherent in the dual roles that people are expected to play helps regulate the interaction among all participants in the scene—an implicit behavioral code of conduct that can be called *karaoke decorum*.

## The Karaoke Decorum

Karaoke decorum involves a set of conventions for maintaining and judging what is to be considered socially appropriate behavior in a karaoke scene. Of course, any such decorum also implies what is inappropriate or socially unacceptable. However, specific karaoke decorum varies from one karaoke setting to another. In advising his Western readers on how to behave in Japanese karaoke bars, Rex Shelley (1993) suggested:

> Karaoke bars can be great fun, or terribly embarrassing. The microphone is on a long lead and when it gets to your table, everyone must do his party thing. Do not try to get out of it by saying that you do not know any Japanese songs. They always have a few popular English language songs in the box to slap down this excuse. "Yesterday" and "My Way" seem to be the top of the karaoke western pops. Do your best. Nobody will really mind if you can't sing provided that you don't sing too long. You cannot refuse. (p. 159)

Ogawa (1993a) offered three other tacit rules in the karaoke space of Japan: One must not sing two songs in succession, one must not sing the same song that the others have sung, and, when others are singing, one must applaud between verses and at the ending of the song.

However, although these rules of decorum may seem standard to those familiar with the Japanese karaoke scene, they are not universally observed. On one Saturday night in May 1994, I witnessed a scene at a Chinese American restaurant in a business area of Washington, DC open for karaoke singing in the late evening. At one point in the evening, two young Taiwanese women together sang two songs in succession. With the exception of their six friends at one table, the two women were singing to an otherwise indifferent audience of about 30 people at four other tables. These other people did not applaud between verses or at the end of the songs, but spent most of the time talking among themselves. Despite this, the night went on without any noticeable unease among the participants in that karaoke scene.

The decorum observed in that Chinese American restaurant undoubtedly differs from the Japanese karaoke decorum that Shelley (1993) and Ogawa (1993a) described so matter-of-factly. In other words, karaoke scene and decorum, as with any other social space and decorum, are culture- or context-bound. Because each dramaturgical web of karaoke necessarily reflects the organizational, material, and symbolic orientation of the people who build and use it, the web may also be said to reflect what Dick Hebdige (1979) defined as the style of that group of people. As I demonstrate later in the book, although karaoke technology varies little from one manufacturer to another, the differing social contexts embodied by the three interpretive communities of Chinese American immigrants that I studied can and do facilitate the construction and maintenance of divergent karaoke scenes and codes of decorum. By extension, they also represent and foster different karaoke experiences, practices, or styles.

## THE ROLE OF PEOPLE IN THE PRODUCTION OF MEANINGS IN KARAOKE SCENES

I already delineated karaoke's dramaturgical web of significance. I now address the question of how karaoke participants can create, maintain, and transform social reality in karaoke scenes; that is, the importance of the karaoke participants in the construction and interpretation of meanings in karaoke scenes. I begin this discussion by examining how the role of the media audience has traditionally been conceptualized.

### Media Audience as Reader

The role of the audience in the reception of media content, or texts, has been a subject of considerable discussion in media and cultural studies.[9] The discussion has mostly been positioned along a theoretical continuum, with the media-centered paradigm located at one end of the continuum and the audience-centered paradigm at the other. Each end of the continuum is described later.

As a somewhat crude illustration of the extremes of media-centered paradigm, the so-called magic bullet theory conjures up an image of the mass media firing powerful messages at, and hitting, the defenseless

---

[9]See, for example, *Critical Studies in Mass Communication's* special issues on "Reading Recent Revisionism" (Thomas, 1990) and "Media Interpretation" (Thomas, 1991) and the *Journal of Communication's* "The Future of the Field II" (Levy, 1993), especially Klaus B. Jensen (1993), Sonia M. Livingstone (1993), and Morley (1993).

audience.[10] This theory suggests that mass media content is fixed and has a direct influence on receivers' knowledge and behavior. "Screen theory" (Moores, 1993) offers an alternative, but equivalent, perspective on the power of the form of the media. Influenced by French poststructuralist theory, and particularly Lacanian psychoanalysis, screen theory argues that how film audiences receive meanings is defined or controlled by the cinematic form or language employed by the filmmakers (Heath, 1977–1978; MacCabe, 1974). Again, the direction of influence is from the medium to the audience.

From the perspective of political economy, critical media studies scholarship offers a comparatively more macroscopic argument by conceptualizing mass media institutions as culture or consciousness industries (Adorno & Horkheimer, 1977; Enzensberger, 1974; Schiller, 1989). Often with cooperation from the state, these industries are said to dominate society with omnipresent, one-dimensional media messages. They limit or drown out alternative voices in the information environment, thereby helping to impose and maintain a hegemonic ideology that favors the state and industry (Ewen, 1976; Garnham, 1990; Marcuse, 1964; Parenti, 1986; Schiller, 1973).[11] From this perspective, people do not have much power to overcome the hegemony fostered and sustained by mainstream media and cultural establishments, unless political and particularly economic changes allow alternative media outlets to flourish.

In contrast, audience-centered critical reception scholarship argues that, to varying degrees, the audience has the ability to interpret and reappropriate in its own terms media texts (Hall, 1980; Morley, 1980; Radway, 1984). Based on semiotic theories, various media and cultural studies scholars argue that media texts involve both aesthetic and social codes (grammars) and are inherently polysemic. A text is said to be polysemic when it can stand for multiple connotations depending on the audience reading (Leeds-Hurwitz, 1993).[12] John Fiske (1987) similarly used the concept of polysemy to suggest that the audience can construct

---

[10]The condition in which this (magic bullet or hypodermic) theory was formulated or the extent to which the theory has ever been formally delineated has received some serious consideration in recent years. See, for example, Bineham (1988) and Sproule (1989).

[11]See also "Ferment in the Field" of the *Journal of Communication* (Gerbner, 1983) for a discussion of critical media studies scholarship. For a recent argument in support of political economy-based analyses of media and culture and some critical responses to the argument, see a special colloquy in *Critical Studies in Mass Communication* (Gandy, 1995).

[12]As opposed to aesthetic and social codes, logical codes are monosemic, that is, the signifier stands for only one signified. As Leeds-Hurwitz (1993) illustrated, "science uses logical codes because the number 4 always stands for the same number of items, whereas my birthday gift to you of a scarf, as part of a social code, implies not only that I remembered your day but equally that I know (or do not know) your preferences in color and fabric" (p. 68).

socially pertinent meanings for themselves with the "semiotic resources provided by television" (p. 65). Linda Steiner (1988) contended that readers of *Ms.* magazine engage in oppositional decoding of various print media messages, including what they consider as insulting advertisements, thus resisting these messages' preferred readings.

Some recent audience reception scholarship has focused more on the constraints placed on the audience by the media system or environment at large. This work represents a midway point on the aforementioned continuum. Dana L. Cloud's (1992) ambivalence thesis, for example, suggests that popular texts "offer viewers a multiplicitous but structured meaning system in which instances of multivocality are complementary parts of the system's overall hegemonic design" (p. 314). In other words, although audience members can be seen as active interpreters of media messages, they do so on the basis of constrained cultural choices. Arnold S. Wolfe (1992) argued that "interpretation is a culturally determined practice rooted in codes shared by message-makers and consumers belonging to the same culture" (p. 272); that is, "[the] meaning of media texts is enabled and constrained by the culture of its origination and completed, even if not created, by its audience" (p. 273).

More recently, John M. Sloop (1994) offered a case study of how various hegemonic social forces can discipline the producers of controversial texts, which he called the "grounds of interpretation." In examining how the rap group Public Enemy—"a voice from the 'margins' of American culture" (p. 345)—was pressured to apologize for and re-present certain anti-Semitic statements made by a band member, Sloop contended that " . . . regardless of how much space audience members have for interpretation or evaluation, 'critical texts' and their producers are encouraged through cultural discipline to become supportive of the dominant ideology rather than resistant to it" (p. 357). In other words, the production of critical media texts can be tempered by dominant cultural forces.

It is important to note that the media texts studied thus far—such as television programs, popular magazines, and romance novels—do not involve their audiences in the process whereby their semiotic resources are produced. If these media texts are what Sloop (1994) called the grounds of interpretation, then audiences are certainly limited in the extent to which they can negotiate meaning because they interpret on the grounds built by others.

Of course, not all traditional mass media products are closed texts in the sense that their semiotic resources cannot be physically altered by the audience during the consumption process. To a certain extent, radio listeners can inject potentially unforeseen information into call-in shows during their calls. Similarly, audience members at rock concerts may affect the outcome of a performance. They can cheer for the performers, thus making the latter more gratified and engaged in their performance.

They can also boo or even throw objects onto the stage, thus upsetting the process of the performance itself.

However, although audience members play a part in injecting unplanned information into these media products, they do not control these products' actual overall planning or production. Indeed, the audience's presence or behavior in the earlier-mentioned or other similar media events is dictated by the events' producers, who have every incentive to protect the interests of their financial or institutional sponsors. Radio producers can and do screen out callers deemed potentially disruptive to the predetermined flow of their program. They beep out callers' unacceptable words. Similarly, police or security personnel are often brought in to rock concerts to prevent any real interference with the show's preset agenda. In other words, the design or construction of the content of these media products is essentially out of the hands of their audience.

In short, this discussion highlights various conceptions of the role that the media audience plays in receiving and interpreting mass media messages. But the discussion to date, particularly in critical audience reception scholarship, tends to focus on analyzing the media audience as readers, mass media products or messages as texts, and audience consumption of mass media products as a process of reading texts. Such a literary perspective in analyzing everyday cultures can be confining. As Carey (1995) argued:

> This is seen most clearly as cultural studies was absorbed into modern language departments and dominated by literary outlooks. For them the study of social phenomena was reduced to interactions with a text—to, however elaborated, an encoding and decoding model . . . . The medium is not the message, nor is it the economy, but the complex interplay between a technology and the entire political, economic, and cultural infrastructure built up in relation to the articulation of a way of life. (p. 84)

Similarly, Moores (1993) provided a thoughtful overview of audience reception scholarship by arguing for the importance and urgency of studying audience consumption of media products in its natural environment, that is, the ethnography of media use. The literary perspective on the audience as readers of media texts, as I demonstrate and argue next, certainly is inadequate in analyzing how media consumers engage in karaoke as a cultural practice. It cannot explain how karaoke participants can and do act as active agents[13] in indigenizing or localizing existing mass-mediated products; that is, appropriate karaoke technology and music in the construction of their personal and social webs of significance.

---

[13]Wong's (1994) study focuses on the role of human agency in the construction of karaoke cultures. See also Lum (1994b).

## From Reading to Production

I suggest that we conceptualize those people who participate in karaoke scenes not just as media consumers who read what they buy from the market (karaoke music) but as producers of the indigenized cultural products (their own karaoke episodes and performances) they at the same time consume. They are producers in two ways. First, they are the ones who plan or organize the karaoke scenes where they are also the performers and audiences. In the karaoke scenes they put together, participants can (and often do) set their own rules or plot the scenes for their own purposes, from the setting and rules of decorum to the specific music versions to be used.[14]

At another level, karaoke participants are the producers of the performances in karaoke scenes. Goffman (1959) referred to performance as "all the activity of an individual which occurs during a period marked by his continuous presence before a particular set of observers and which has some influence on the observers" (p. 22). Performances are the actual, lived acts, events, and situations that are the substance of human interaction (Bauman & Sherzer, 1989; Hymes, 1975) that help establish, revise, and eventually maintain interactional structure in the context of everyday life (Leeds-Hurwitz, Sigman, & Sullivan, 1995). Thus, karaoke performers—both singers and audience members—literally produce or create their scenes with each other.

There are two categories of performance in a karaoke scene. The first category is the participants' activity while interacting with others in the audience area. The second is the activity of engaging with karaoke music in the stage area. I discussed earlier most of the basic dramaturgical elements that help construct karaoke scenes. I now turn to the specific role of karaoke music in constructing the performance in the stage area.

In and of itself, karaoke music or songs are incomplete in their content—by definition, an orchestra without the lead vocal. Karaoke music is designed to be reprocessed, to be interwoven with live vocals.[15] Of course, the karaoke music producers have already set up in their studio the musical-technical parameters that their consumers can or are expected to perform within. In addition, many karaoke performers do try to sing "cover" (Fornäs, 1994, p. 92)—that is, imitate or conform to the musical-technical specificities of the original music.

---

[14]For legal or financial reasons, karaoke music producers normally do not use the master sound tracks by the original artists. Instead, they hire their own performers to reproduce or imitate the original music. As a result, there can be as many versions of one song as there are software producers. Some people who are used to one particular version of a song may not like or be able to sing renditions by other producing groups.

[15]One can watch a music video on a karaoke laserdisc with its vocal track on, but that is an act of watching video, in much the same way as one watches any prerecorded video or music video on MTV. It does not constitute a karaoke scene.

However, that is just one of a variety of ways in which people approach karaoke performance. To some people, singing karaoke is but one way to congregate with people whose company they enjoy. They really do not care much if they can sing well at all. As James, a young professional at a pharmaceutical company in New Jersey, told me at the end of a private karaoke party, "Since all of us are amateurs and we will never beat the pros like Lau Tak-Hwa [a popular singer in Hong Kong], we should then just do our best, be ourselves, enjoy ourselves. To express ourselves is the most important thing."

Similarly, there are people who for various reasons deliberately change the words of the songs they sing. I observed how Peter, an employee of Richard and Diane's, presented himself at their party mentioned at the beginning of this chapter. It was known among the couple's employees that Richard and Diane held opposing views of Peter; Richard did not like Peter, whereas Diane did. In singing Elvis' "The Hawaiian Wedding Song," Peter changed the lines "I love *you* with all my heart" (to "I love *my boss* with all my heart") and "Promise me that you will *leave* me never" (to "Promise me that you will *fire* me never"). All the while, Peter turned to Richard, who was sitting comfortably in his couch, but who did not seem to pay much attention to what Peter was doing.

In other words, there is no telling prior to the performance how karaoke's prepackaged music will eventually sound when the music is mixed with live vocals or, for that matter, how participants will respond to the final outcome. Equally important, karaoke music is meant to be integrated as part of a larger event. It represents just one of the many audiovisual elements or semiotic resources that make up a performance on stage. People's costume, makeup, style and competence of presentation, persona, reputation, and so forth, are as important as their choice of music in packaging their performance in the stage area.[16] Because the production of karaoke performances involves the audience in a live environment—unlike the production of any other traditional mass media—the cultural projects of karaoke are by nature dynamic, hybrid, and intensely indigenous. Accordingly, the interpretation of the social and cultural significance of karaoke's performances can often be difficult, unpredictable, and volatile.

## The Site of Significance

Given an understanding of the nature of karaoke's cultural productions—that is, the construction of and the performances in karaoke

---

[16]In his study of a sample of karaoke scenes in Taiwan, Ringo Ma (1994) suggested that a performer's reputation and regional background can play a role in determining how the audience will react to the performance.

scenes—we must confront the question of how significance or meaning may be derived from these projects. What are the grounds of interpretation? To address this question, I utilize Stanley Fish's (1980) interpretive communities approach as my conceptual frame, for three reasons. First, the field research on which this book is based indicates that people who congregate in similar dramaturgical sites tend to share social, economic, and ethnic backgrounds. Second, people who congregate in their preferred karaoke scenes tend to utilize karaoke to similar ends. Third, as suggested earlier, people congregating in karaoke scenes play an active role in the construction and appropriation of meanings.

An interpretive community is the sum of people who experience a text according to a frame of reference commonly shared among them. An interpretive community shares a set of assumptions resulting from prior knowledge, experience, values, beliefs, and expectations (Fish, 1980). In its original theoretical context, the interpretive communities thesis was posited to shed light on the active role that a reader plays in generating meaning while engaging a literary work. As Fish (1980) argued:

> If meaning is embedded in the text, the reader's responsibilities are limited to the job of getting it out; but if meaning develops, and if it develops in a dynamic relationship with the reader's expectations, projections, conclusions, judgments, and assumptions, these activities (the things that reader *does*) are not merely instrumental, or mechanical, but essential, and the act of description must both begin and end with them. (pp. 2–3)

Any meaning deemed significant to members of the community, therefore, is not a static entity prepackaged by the author into the text itself. Instead, it is the outcome of an ongoing process of interpretation of what is presented in the text through the looking glass of the reader's frame of reference. Presumably, then, readers with different frames of reference will generate divergent meanings from even a single text. People who share a similar frame of reference and set of interpretations for a text, then, constitute an interpretive community.

But we have to be cautious in using Fish's interpretive communities approach to conceptualize the sense-making experience of karaoke participants. We cannot claim that karaoke participants have some sort of formal interpretive strategies in the same way Fish speaks of the interpretive strategies employed by, for instance, Marxist, Freudian, or Jungian literary critics. Similarly, we cannot equate a karaoke audience's strategy to Ludwik Fleck's (1979) thought style or Thomas S. Kuhn's (1970) paradigm, as the latter two concepts, in their original contexts, are used to describe the sets of formal procedures that scientists employ to frame and understand their subjects. Fish's interpretive strategy, Fleck's thought style, and Kuhn's paradigm are the result of direct, explicit, and systematic training. Karaoke participants, on the other hand, do not have any such formal training for constructing their interpretive strategies.

However, people do bring years of experience in communicating with others, especially those like themselves, to karaoke scenes. This is the set of social, economic, political, and cultural conditions that they are socialized into; and the collective as well as individual ways of doing things they acquire in response to these conditions. Communication, as Wendy Leeds-Hurwitz (1989) reminded us, is a learned behavior. Through informal socialization, or what E. Weinstein (1969) called incidental learning, people acquire the rules and skills necessary for interacting with others and in the process become part of a community.

In addressing the role of communication in community building, John Dewey (1916) suggested:

> There is more than a verbal tie between the words common, community, and communication. Men live in a community in virtue of the things which they have in common; and communication is the way in which they come to possess things in common. What they must have in common . . . are aims, beliefs, aspirations, knowledge—a common under-standing—likemindedness as sociologists say. (pp. 5–6)

The likemindedness among people gives them the identity of being members of a community. It is this likemindedness among people that forms their common frame of reference to construct and comprehend their social and cultural reality. As Jensen (1990) elaborated on the interpretive communities approach:

> It should be emphasized that interpretive communities represent an analytical perspective that complements rather than substitutes for socioeconomic categories. First, the word *interpretive* implies that audiences, while being demographic entities, also make up cultural formations, whose interpretive strategies in relation to mass media give rise to different constructions of social reality. The relationship between cultural and demographic formations is not well understood. Second, the word *communities* indicates that audiences may also constitute social agents with shared interests, or publics. (p. 130)

What I am suggesting is that, despite its literary roots, the interpretive communities approach can be used to conceptualize how people's common social and economic characteristics may play a role in their conceiving, producing, and ultimately making sense of their own karaoke experiences as both producer and audience. Therefore, in the context of this book, I am reframing Fish's (1980) interpretive communities approach as a social and cultural rather than as a literary project. In doing so, I suggest that I must also locate karaoke practices in their specific social and cultural location, where several interpretive communities of Chinese American immigrants have spun their karaoke dramaturgical webs.

In the next chapter, before I begin my presentation and analysis of the divergent karaoke experiences of the three interpretive communities of first-generation Chinese American immigrants I encountered during fieldwork, I examine in historical and sociological terms how karaoke can be analyzed as part of the overall media experience of the Chinese diaspora in the United States. Therefore, chapter 2 is a continuation of the discussion in this current chapter, where I have analyzed karaoke as a technological embodiment of certain cultural practices of amateur, communal singing, and the indispensable role of the participants in the construction of social reality or meanings in everyday contexts.

The remainder of the book is organized as follows. Chapters 3, 4, and 5 analyze the use of karaoke in three Chinese American immigrant communities. The analysis in these chapters reveals the differing meanings and uses of karaoke technology and participation across the communities. These divergent meanings and uses are related to contrasting life circumstances of members of the three communities. Chapter 6 summarizes the data and places them within a larger theoretical context that is concerned with the immigrant experience in the United States and the role of interactive media technology in people's construction of their social and cultural identities.

# 2

# Media in the
# Chinese American Experience:
# The Formation and
# Media/tion of the Diaspora

The mass media play an important role in the social and cultural life of immigrants in the United States. At the turn of the 20th century, such prominent scholars as Charles Cooley (1909), Dewey (1916), and Robert Park (1920, 1925) began to reflect on the relationship between the press and the immigrant experience. Park (1922), for example, examined the role that the foreign-language press played in facilitating or inhibiting the assimilation and Americanization of immigrants. Most of the immigrants that Park (1922) examined had been peasants in Europe. These early immigrants were drawn to the immigrant press because they were not allowed to have their own press while at home for political reasons. Living in the United States, they acquired the freedom to read and produce information of their choice, including information to keep them in touch with their homelands or help them adjust to their adopted country.

The work by Park and his contemporaries in studying the immigrant press helped initiate the discussion of how the mass media can be used and analyzed as a means for the expression, maintenance, transformation, or any combination of these traits of diasporic cultures and communities. These early works can also help us conceptualize the role that the media play in establishing a voice for Chinese immigrants in the United States and helping them maintain a link to their old cultures.

Indeed, the role of karaoke in the articulation of part of Chinese American immigrant culture has to be viewed in the context of the overall development of Chinese American media. This chapter presents a historical and sociological discussion of how Chinese American karaoke can and should be understood as part of the overall media experience in the Chinese diaspora.

## CHINESE-LANGUAGE MEDIA IN THE OLD DAYS

The development of Chinese-language media has gone hand in hand with the evolution of the Chinese diaspora. At the time of Cooley's (1909), Dewey's (1916), and Park's (1920, 1922, 1925) writings, Chinese America was by all measures a very small place. Discriminatory immigration policies had kept the size of the Chinese American population small. To exclude Chinese laborers, Congress enacted the Chinese Exclusion Act in 1882—just 3 years before the Statue of Liberty was constructed in New York harbor. The Chinese Exclusion Act became the first and only federal law ever to exclude a group of people by nationality or race (Kwong, 1987). It suspended the immigration of Chinese laborers for 10 years, deported illegal entrants, and denied existing Chinese immigrants the right to become naturalized citizens (Mark & Chih, 1982).

A host of similar laws was also put into place in subsequent years.[1] For a long time, early Chinese immigrants, known in the immigrant community itself as *lou hwakiu* (or "old overseas Chinese"), were not permitted to bring their families with them. In 1890, the Chinese male-to-female ratio in the United States was 27 to 1 (Lee, 1960, cited in Kwong, 1987; see also Wong, 1985). The Chinese American population dropped from 105,465 in 1880 to 85,202 in 1920 (Hing, 1993). In 1943, six decades after its enactment, the Chinese Exclusion Act was finally repealed. China's ally status during World War II had produced some good will in the United States toward Chinese people. Nevertheless, only a minuscule quota of 105 Chinese immigrants was admitted annually (Kwong, 1987).

As newcomers in their adopted country, and because of the language barrier, many of these *lou hwakiu* had tended to gravitate toward their compatriots for mutual support. At the same time, overt and often violent racial hostility in the United States effectively kept the *lou hwakiu* in social and economic enclaves, which later came to be known

---

[1]Fourteen additional pieces of anti-Chinese legislation were passed in the decades following 1882 (Mark & Chih, 1982). For more detailed treatments on discriminatory legislative actions against Chinese immigrants in particular, see Sucheng Chan (1991) and against various Asian immigrant groups in general, see Bill Ong Hing (1993). In 1924, a discriminatory national origins provision in the immigration law was enacted with the expressed purpose of preserving what was considered by the approving lawmakers to be the racial and ethnic character of the United States. As a result of this provision, according to Peter Kwong (1987), "94 percent of immigration quotas were assigned to the countries of Northern and Western Europe" (p. 21). Although Chinese immigration was prohibited between 1882 and 1943, temporary entry visas were issued to certain Chinese, such as merchants, government representatives, and students (Kwong, 1987). Moreover, those who claimed derivative U.S. citizenship, that is, they were born to U.S. citizens, could also bypass the Exclusion Act. See Ronald Takaki (1989) for a discussion of how some Chinese falsely claimed status in this category and later became known as "paper sons" in gaining entry into the United States.

as Chinatowns (Kwong, 1987; Pan, 1990).[2] In 1898, the Chinatown in New York City, which some of the *lou hwakiu* in the United States called their home, consisted of only several narrow streets. They included Mott, Pell, Doyer, Bayard, and Baxter Streets; and Chatham Square, a few blocks south of the Manhattan Bridge (Chen, 1993). With a degree of awkwardness in hindsight but not without insight, Park wrote in 1922 that the Chinese were part of the so-called "exotics" because "they are or seem to be, more completely isolated and removed from contact and participation in American life than any other immigrant peoples" (p. 290).

In their isolation from the hostility in the host society, the majority of *lou hwakiu* formed close-knit social networks with compatriots from similar ethnic backgrounds. Personal networks were essential for the survival of these early Chinese immigrants. Many of them came from rural areas in Toishan and other parts of the Kwangtung Province, where Canton is the capital. To those *lou hwakiu* who came from humble backgrounds and were not proficiently literate, oral or face-to-face communication was a vital process for obtaining information and for relating to others.

Moreover, not unlike people from other ethnic groups, many Chinese people were conscious about their regional background as an important part of their ethnicity. Elsewhere (Lum, 1994a), I have suggested that, to a large extent, every Chinese person has a double identity. The first is the ethnic identity of being Chinese in the most general sense of the word, particularly in contrast to people from other ethnic groups. At the intraethnic level, however, every Chinese has a regional identity—for example, as a Cantonese or Toishanese, that is, a Chinese from Canton or Toishan, respectively.

Regionalism is a factor that helps define how many Chinese relate and identify among themselves. It certainly played an important role in how the social networks in old Chinatowns across the United States and in other overseas Chinese communities were established, such as district or same-surname associations (Wong, 1985). Not only did these organizations provide their members with a place to socialize, they also offered *lou hwakiu* an array of other services, such as job or business referrals or the settling of family or community disputes.

By the same token, Chinese-language newspapers served as a handy source of information for those who were literate in Chinese. Reading the news in their own language certainly helped these people to navigate in the unfamiliar waters of their adopted country. As Park (1922) put it, "news is a kind of urgent information that men use in making adjustments to a new environment, in changing old habits, and in forming new

---

[2]The bitter experience of early Chinese immigrants in the United States was also shared by many other Asian immigrants (Takaki, 1989).

opinions" (p. 9). The Chinese-language press, as with other immigrant presses, also informed its readers of their old country and reminded them of their old customs and cultures. In this regard, it gave its readers what Tsan-Kuo Chang (1983) called a linkage to the past and a forum where they can have a voice of their own.

## CHANGES AFTER 1965

It was not until the enactment of the 1965 Immigration Act that the social as well as the media ecology of Chinese America began to evolve drastically. The Immigration Act of 1965 helped transform the social, economic, and political structure of old Chinatowns across the United States and Asian America in general (Hing, 1993; Min, 1994). In effect, it repealed most of the prior discriminatory immigration policies by allowing a flat annual quota of 20,000 immigrants from every country in the Eastern Hemisphere into the United States.[3]

As a beneficiary of the 1965 Immigration Act, the Chinese American population rapidly rose from 237,272 in 1960 to 435,062 in 1970, and from 806,027 in 1980 (United States Bureau of Census compiled by Wang and cited in Mark & Chih, 1982) to 1,079,400 in 1985 (Kwong, 1987). By 1980, the number of foreign-born Chinese represented 63.3% of the overall Chinese American population, and between 1980 and 1990 almost 446,000 Chinese immigrated to the United States (Hing, 1993). In the 1990 census, there were 1,645,472 documented Chinese in the United States, 238,919 of whom were in New York City alone (United States Bureau of Census, 1990, enumerated by Doyle & Khandelwal, 1993). These numbers, of course, do not include illegal immigrants nor those who did not participate in the census.[4]

Equally important, not only did the 1965 Immigration Act bring in more Chinese immigrants, it also brought in Chinese immigrants from much more diverse backgrounds. About 70% of the Chinese who came to the United States in accordance with the 1965 Immigration Act were the families of *lou hwakiu,* who mostly came from a homogeneous and humble agrarian background in Toishan and its vicinities in the Kwangtung Province. These immigrants tended to settle in Chinatowns across the country (Kwong, 1987).

---

[3]China and Taiwan have been granted separate quotas since 1982.

[4]An Immigration and Naturalization Service report estimated that there were about 24,200 illegal Chinese immigrants in the United States; slightly more than one half of this national total (12,700) was thought to be in New York State (Sontag, 1993). Because these estimates were made based on the discrepancy between the number of Chinese entering the country and the number of Chinese leaving the country with a visa or passport, the estimates do not include those who entered the United States through other means, such as smuggling.

The remaining portion of the annual quota, however, was maintained to attract people with professional skills. This latter group of new immigrants tended to come from more diverse regional, educational, socioeconomic, and linguistic backgrounds (Chen, 1992; Hing, 1993; Min, 1994). According to Diane Mei Lin Mark and Ginger Chih (1982), many of the post-1965 Chinese immigrants from this latter category were professionals "whose high level of education and good spoken English gained them good jobs and homes in the suburbs" (p. 111) or, more simply, outside of Chinatowns. Some of these immigrants first came as foreign college or graduate students and later acquired their degrees and citizenship.

Meanwhile, economic prosperity and continued political uncertainty in China, Hong Kong, and Taiwan have accelerated the export of human resources and financial investments from these regions into the United States. As the influx of these new resources and investments further the growth of local Chinese American economies across the country (Zhou, 1992), the social and cultural ecology of Chinese immigrant communities is also beginning to change drastically. For example, the 1970s and 1980s saw the migration of many Chinese immigrants from Chinatown in Manhattan into the outer boroughs and suburbs of the New York and New Jersey metropolitan area. U. S. Census Bureau figures indicate that in 1990, almost 70% of the Chinese population in New York City lived outside Manhattan, notably in Queens and Brooklyn. In the same year, New Jersey recorded a total of 59,084 Chinese in its census, up from 23,369 in 1980.

The rapid increase of Chinese immigrants created a substantial audience base to sustain the growth of Chinese-language mass media. The new immigrants helped expand the size of the reading public in the Chinese communities across the country. Coming from rich media-producing areas such as Hong Kong and Taiwan, these immigrants also brought high expectations for the quality of the media products they consumed, as well as for the extent of their media consumption. The dispersion of these immigrants from urban enclaves, such as China-towns, to the suburbs also helped spur the development of Chinese-language electronic mass media.

Beginning in the 1970s, several Chinese-language radio and television programs slowly emerged in cities with large Chinese immigrant settlements, such as New York City (Cheng, 1990), Los Angeles (Lin, 1990), and San Francisco (Chang, 1990). The 1980s then witnessed the rapid expansion and professionalization of Chinese-language media (Lum, 1996). The news content of print, cable, and broadcast (UHF) media has come to include local, national, and international sources (Lii, 1995; Lum, 1991). Chinese-language television programs and prerecorded videotapes feature dramas or variety specials of exceptional production values from Hong Kong and Taiwan and, to a lesser extent,

China. Early in 1995, TVB Satellite, an international arm of Television Broadcast, Ltd. in Hong Kong, began direct satellite broadcast of Chinese-language television programming on a 24-hour, 7-day-a-week basis to paying viewers equipped with a special reception system.

In short, the media ecology of Chinese America has gradually become more sophisticated and competitive in the three decades since the 1965 Immigration Act. This Act helped transform the social, economic, and ethnic composition of Chinese America. It is in this context that karaoke has emerged as one of the newest media forms and cultural practices that give many Chinese Americans a link to their past, as well as a forum where they can have a voice of their own.

## KARAOKE COMES TO CHINESE AMERICA

To a certain extent, the development of Chinese-language media in the United States immigrant communities follows in the footsteps of media development in Hong Kong, Taiwan, and China. Many of the media businesses, products, and services taking hold or available in New York's Chinese immigrant communities are imported from these regions. Immigrants and business investors from these regions often are the sources for the diffusion of Chinese-language media within the United States. The emergence and diffusion of karaoke in Chinese America reflects this general trend.

The second half of the 1980s saw the rapidly growing popularity of karaoke in various parts of Asia, including Taiwan (Li, 1992; Li 1993), Hong Kong (Lin & Lu, 1992), and China (Lu, 1992; Ming, 1992). In recalling the spread of karaoke in Hong Kong, Kenny Lau (personal communication, August 15, 1993), a General Manager in the Hong Kong office of Polygram Records, a leading karaoke software producer in Asia, observed:

> In the beginning, karaoke appeared only in karaoke "lounges." Then karaoke appeared in discos, hotels, restaurants, clubs, and many other entertainment establishments. Karaoke is now a must to attract customers, especially in discos and restaurants; they can't exist without a karaoke system. People want karaoke in these places besides eating or dancing. *It has gradually become a culture, something "invisible," something people have taken for granted. It indeed has become part of many people's lives.* In the beginning, only those who used to go out at night or those who went to the lounges went to sing karaoke. Then everybody went to karaoke. All ages, different types of people from different backgrounds. Some companies even produce Cantonese opera songs in karaoke now, for old people. (italics added)

As karaoke has become a cultural practice in Hong Kong and other parts of Asia, it is also being exported to overseas Chinese communities around the world. New York's Chinatown is one such community where karaoke has become a cultural influence in the everyday lives of many people. The following description examines the initial infusion of karaoke into the Chinese immigrant communities in New York City.

### An Early Chinese American Karaoke Restaurant

One of the earliest known Chinese restaurants in New York City that featured a specially designed karaoke facility in the dining room was Seven By Seven. Located on Houston Street on the Lower West Side of Manhattan, it went into business early in 1988. According to Philip Chin, one of the restaurant's seven initial partners, Seven By Seven was intended to be a karaoke club (personal communication, July 5, 1994), but the partners eventually decided to change it to a restaurant featuring karaoke and a bar, assuming the new arrangement would bring in more business.[5]

Seven By Seven occupied about 2,000 square feet with a maximum capacity of about 100 people. Next to the bar was the dining area with a small stage, about 6 feet by 10 feet, set against a wall. A karaoke disc jockey room was placed next to the kitchen. The karaoke system was a cassette tape-based system (which would be considered primitive only a few years later, in the early 1990s, when laserdisc-based systems became the standard). The tape selection contained mostly Cantonese songs, because the majority of customers at Seven by Seven were Hong Kong Cantonese immigrants from the nearby Chinatown. There were some Mandarin songs (a Taiwanese partner had brought in some Mandarin-speaking customers) and a small number of English songs. Customers sang their chosen songs with the help of a songbook.

The restaurant opened 7 days a week from 11 a.m. until 4 a.m. the next morning. Friday and Saturday were the busiest days of the week, usually drawing a full house. The restaurant was normally half full at the other times. There were not too many people during dinner hours though. In other words, most of the people who patronized the restaurant were attracted not to its food but to karaoke. Customers coming for karaoke usually arrived after 9 or 10 in the evening, after dinner or a movie. Most of the customers who stayed between 10 p.m. and 1 a.m. were younger people, usually in their 20s. Those who came after midnight tended to be older, in their 30s, and often included more restaurant workers and *daailou* ("big brother," one of many slang terms in Canton-

---

[5]Most of the partners of Seven By Seven had full-time jobs elsewhere. Chin, for example, was a technician at a utility company during the day at the time the restaurant was established. He was a student of mine in a video workshop I taught for a nonprofit organization in New York's Chinatown early in the 1980s.

ese referring to gangsters). Chin recalled that customers at the restaurant were usually orderly when the night was still young, but occasional fistfights started to occur after midnight, especially when the restaurant was crowded and some of the customers were drunk. Seven by Seven lasted for about a year and a half.

In the subsequent years, more and more Chinese restaurants and clubs offered karaoke as an attraction. Thus, by the early 1990s, karaoke had become a fixture in all kinds of eating, drinking, and entertainment establishments in New York metropolitan Chinese immigrant communities. This is similar to the Hong Kong experience described earlier. However, as I have already suggested, because contemporary Chinese immigrants to the United States come from diverse social, economic, educational, and regional backgrounds, their expectations of and experience with karaoke differ. The divergent character of the karaoke experience is detailed next and in the remainder of this study.

### THREE INTERPRETIVE COMMUNITIES OF CHINESE AMERICAN KARAOKE

As previously noted (see chap. 1), karaoke encapsulates certain cultural practices of amateur participatory singing whereby social reality can be created, maintained, and transformed. How karaoke is ultimately used and the social consequences of such usage are determined by the past experiences, needs, and expectations of the people who use it; as well as by the interactional performance making use of it; hence the concept of the interpretive communities of karaoke. To contextualize Chinese American karaoke practices in this ethnography, earlier in this chapter I examined in historical and sociological terms the role of media in the Chinese American experience. Karaoke, along with other Chinese-language media before it, should be analyzed as part of the articulation of Chinese immigrant cultures in the United States.

Chapters 3, 4, and 5 present the karaoke experiences of three interpretive communities of first-generation Chinese American immigrants in the greater New York–New Jersey metropolitan area. The focus of my analysis is on how these interpretive communities of immigrants use karaoke as a forum for the construction of their respective social identities. In regard to their relationship with karaoke, people across these communities share certain similarities. For example, most of these people began to participate in social singing only after the introduction of karaoke into their lives. Similarly, they all now sing karaoke as a form of entertainment.

However, members of these three interpretive communities of first-generation immigrants also evidence certain differences in how they engage karaoke as a cultural practice that articulates aspects of their personal and social lives. Based on original data I gathered from field research (see Appendix), chapters 3, 4, and 5 develop three distinct themes: karaoke as cultural connection and translation, karaoke as status symbol, and karaoke as escape, respectively, to describe the different uses and significance of karaoke to the three communities.

The first interpretive community consists of mostly lower middle to middle-class Cantonese people from Hong Kong and its vicinities in southern China. Members of this group are socially active in New York's Chinatown on the Lower East Side of Manhattan. Although their main interest is in singing Cantonese opera songs, these people use karaoke as an alternative medium for Cantonese opera singing for themselves and for providing cultural service to the elderly in their ethnic community. Chapter 3 examines the interaction between two cultural forms, karaoke singing and Cantonese opera singing, and the theoretical as well as social and cultural implications of this interaction. Specifically, the analysis focuses on how members of this interpretive community adopt karaoke as a means of cultural connection and, in the process, how Cantonese opera music is translated into karaoke.

The second interpretive community I studied consists mostly of Taiwanese immigrants. Coming from affluent backgrounds, members of this community are highly educated professionals living in exclusive neighborhoods in New Jersey. They adopt an interpretive frame of reference that views karaoke as a status symbol. Chapter 4 examines how karaoke is used by people in this affluent interpretive community as a means to express their wealth and social class and, to a certain extent, their individual competitive drive.

The third interpretive community, whose members are mostly Malaysians of Chinese descent living in the Flushing area of Queens in New York City, is examined in chapter 5. Most of the members in this community come from humble backgrounds. Many of these people are undocumented immigrants and are therefore confined to the economic underground. To many members of this community, karaoke serves as a temporary form of escape. The chapter examines how these people create a socially therapeutic mechanism around karaoke because the humdrum existence of their everyday life is diminished.

There are two clarifications to be made. First, it is important to note that, by analyzing the interpretive communities with regard to the three themes, I do not suggest that the three uses of karaoke are exclusive to the respective communities. At one level, karaoke can certainly be considered a form of cultural connection for many people other than those in the first interpretive community outlined in this study. A substantial portion of the karaoke repertoire in general contains old songs, thus allowing users of all ages to be in touch with popular (and in some cases traditional) music from older generations. To a certain extent, it is also true that many people across the communities and beyond can use karaoke to express their wealth or social status. Karaoke clubs in Hong Kong, for example, are ranked by some according to their degrees of luxury and, correspondingly, by the kinds of rich and famous people who frequent them (Karaoke, 1993). At yet another level, one may argue that anyone can use karaoke as a form of escape. It is not an uncommon sentiment among many people that they like to sing karaoke because it allows them to feel like "a star" (Ban, 1991) or to attain temporary relief from the stress sustained at work (Wu, 1993).

However, as the following three data chapters indicate, the three themes highlighted are characteristic of how people in the respective interpretive communities of Chinese American immigrants engage and experience karaoke. Because they have to constantly negotiate between singing Cantonese opera songs with traditional musical arrangements and the karaoke form, karaoke as cultural connection and translation has become the defining theme for many Hong Kong Cantonese in the first community. Similarly, because social and material attainment is at the center of their karaoke experience, karaoke as status symbol has manifested itself as the dominant theme in how people in the affluent Taiwanese interpretive community engage karaoke. Finally, because gaining mutual comfort and relief from everyday loneliness and hardship is at the core of their karaoke practices, karaoke as escape has emerged as the primary theme in how the many Malaysian Chinese in the third interpretive community embrace karaoke.

On the other hand, and this is the second clarification, it is important to emphasize that I do not in any way suggest a requisite correlation between the socioeconomic experience and the ethnic, regional, or national background of the people being portrayed. The affluence and cultural pluralism enjoyed by those Taiwanese in chapter 4 is shared by many first-generation immigrants from Hong Kong and Malaysia and, for that matter, from other parts of the world. By the same token, the experience of many of the Malaysian Chinese in chapter 5 does not represent the whole spectrum of experiences of all Malaysian Chinese in the United States. The experience of being entrapped in oppressive immigrant enclaves is not unique only among people in this community. Many Chinese immigrants from various other regional backgrounds and, for that matter, many immigrants in the United States who come from a great variety of other nationalities and ethnicities certainly share the same fate.

Nevertheless, there is some connection between the material and economic circumstances of members of each community and how they view and use karaoke technology in scenes of their own creation. I base my final analysis on the implications of these immigrants' karaoke experiences on our understanding of the cultural adaptation of communication technology, audience interaction with electronic media, and media in the Chinese American experience (chap. 6). The issues of ethnicity, gender, and class are the focus of this final analysis of the partial role of karaoke in the three interpretive communities' Chinese American experience.

# 3

# Karaoke as Cultural Connection and Translation: The Voice of a Hong Kong Cantonese Community in New York's Chinatown

This chapter analyzes the karaoke experience of the first interpretive community in this study. Similar to Chinese-language media before it, karaoke is here viewed as a link between some first-generation Chinese immigrants and their indigenous cultures back home. This link can be viewed at two levels. At the general level, karaoke is used by these immigrants as a way to partake of certain cultural products, such as songs and video images, from their homeland. At the second and more specific level, karaoke is used by these immigrants to engage in an older cultural practice, that is, Cantonese opera singing. The next section provides an overview of the social, economic, and ethnic background of people in this interpretive community—by way of introducing one of the community's most defining rituals. The remaining sections of the chapter discuss how karaoke is used by members of this community as cultural connection and translation.

## CANTONESE OPERA SINGING AT THE MID-AUTUMN FESTIVAL

Mrs. Chung is among the thousands upon thousands of Hong Kong Cantonese who emigrated to New York's Chinatown after 1965. Like many of her contemporaries, Mrs. Chung is also caught up in karaoke, but the way she and her friends engage in karaoke is quite noteworthy. Indeed, Mrs. Chung first came to my attention in a brief community affairs announcement in a Chinese newspaper early in the fall of 1993.

In it, she noted that a street party for people in the neighborhood would be held at a certain location in Chinatown. It was a karaoke singing party to celebrate the Mid-Autumn Festival.

According to folk legend, the Mid-Autumn Festival, on the 15th day of the eighth lunar month (early to mid-September in the Gregorian calendar), is the day people in agrarian China celebrate the final harvest of the year. It is believed that the *Toudei Gung* (Earth God) was born on this day, when the moon, a symbol of heaven, is at its roundest and brightest. The festival is therefore a time for people to express their gratitude to heaven and earth for the blessings they have enjoyed during the past year (Hu, 1994). Eating moon cakes and moon gazing are among the festival's many customs (Hu, 1990). Because the roundness of the moon symbolizes family unity and closeness, the festival is also an occasion for family reunion. Similarly, lovers meet and pray on this day for eternal togetherness.

People who have loved ones to experience the holiday with enjoy the Mid-Autumn Festival. On the other hand, those who are displaced or not in love may not have the same cheerful feeling toward the occasion, just as an American with no family to speak of may feel quite lonely on Thanksgiving Day. It was for this reason that Mrs. Chung specifically mentioned in her newspaper announcement that she would welcome senior citizens. She has had frequent contacts with senior citizens at a social center for the elderly in Chinatown where she volunteers. Many of the elderly people with whom Mrs. Chung has contact no longer have a family, or, for a variety of reasons, their family is not with them most of the time.

In addition, there is no official holiday in the United States for Chinese festivals, including the Chinese Lunar New Year. Most of the younger people in the working-class families in the neighborhood would likely have been either at work or in school during the day. "Those *louyanga* are always lonesome," Mrs. Chung said to me in an interview, "I feel sad for them." (*Louyanga* is a polite term in Cantonese used to address elderly people.) Mrs. Chung wanted to create a special event to *ginglou* (respect the elderly). She wanted to add a few joyful moments for those *louyanga* who might not have much to do on this occasion.

Mrs. Chung organized two such Mid-Autumn Festival karaoke parties in 1993 and 1994. What was interesting about Mrs. Chung's karaoke parties was that they did not feature the singing of popular songs, the mainstay of karaoke music. Instead, the parties emphasized Cantonese opera songs. Anyone in the audience interested in singing chose from Mrs. Chung's collection of songs. Those who, for whatever reasons, chose not to sing could enjoy the performance by others.

Mr. Hau, Mrs. Chung's business associate, was the master of ceremonies. An enthusiast of Cantonese opera singing in his mid-40s, Mr. Hau encouraged people in the audience to sing, but only about 10 to 12 people out of several dozen in the audience eventually performed. Most of these performers were Mrs. Chung and Mr. Hau's friends, also enthusiasts of Cantonese opera singing. These people came from a background similar to Mrs. Chung's: mostly Cantonese from Hong Kong and its vicinities, arriving in the United States in the last three decades. Among these people were small-business owners, factory and office workers, technicians, sales clerks, and some retirees. Most of them came to the United States when they were relatively young. As I argue next, these compatriots of Mrs. Chung form a distinct interpretive community and approach karaoke similarly.

## A Community Where the Past and the Present Meet

Lily, as Mrs. Chung is also known among her friends in the community, came to New York's Chinatown with her family some 30 years ago. "I was still a daughter then," Mrs. Chung said. In the first years after Lily's arrival, New York's Chinatown was still a small ethnic community. In 1970, there were only 81,378 Chinese in all of New York State (Zhou, 1992). "You wouldn't see many Chinese on Bowery near Canal Street after about eleven in the morning, after many of them had gone to work either in Uptown or somewhere upstate," Mrs. Chung recalled. Of course, what she said did not deny the fact that many Chinese residents were also hard at work in Chinatown's local businesses.

After years of working in Chinatown, Mrs. Chung and her husband saved enough money to buy the five-story walk-up apartment building on the outskirts of Chinatown where she eventually held the karaoke parties. Mrs. Chung's entrepreneurial drive never seemed to subside, even after many years of working hard every day. In the storefront of her building, she had a business that provided various services for people in the community, such as rent collection, tax return filing, and immigration applications.

Mrs. Chung and many of her contemporaries are some of the many people who have helped to keep what Min Zhou (1992) considered the "enclave economy" of New York's Chinatown as a thriving enterprise. Some of the people, however, work outside the Chinatown area. Many of the people in this network are bilingual in Cantonese and English, although many of those who are in their 40s to late 50s are less fluent in English. Mostly in their mid-30s to early 50s, people in this community are socially active in New York's Chinatown, despite often living in the outer boroughs, particularly in Queens and Brooklyn.

What defines Mrs. Chung and people like her as members of an interpretive community is their common passion for singing Cantonese opera, and how this common passion has helped define the ways in which they engage karaoke. Their experience illustrates how an old cultural practice can be translated and adopted in a new media form and also illustrates the social role played by this new form in these people's everyday lives. Before analyzing the process of translation and adoption of Cantonese opera music into the karaoke form, the next section takes a closer look at the social and cultural functions of Cantonese opera.

## IN TOUCH WITH AN OLD CULTURE

The formation of this interpretive community began when people like Mrs. Chung crossed paths with one another through several Cantonese opera musical associations in New York's Chinatown. Like Mrs. Chung, Jennifer had never pictured herself singing Cantonese opera songs (or *yutkuk*) before coming to New York City, where she worked for a bank in Chinatown. She used to dislike Cantonese opera when she was in Hong Kong in the 1970s. "The drums were too noisy," Jennifer once complained to me.

In addition, like many of those who were more in tune with Western-style popular culture, Jennifer often thought of Cantonese opera as an old people's thing, something that only people from her parents' and grandparents' generations would love to see and hear. The suggestion Kenny Lau of Polygram Records made in chapter 2—that software developers produce Cantonese opera songs in karaoke for old people—reveals the age stereotype associated with Cantonese opera. Like many teenagers in Hong Kong, Jennifer preferred listening to popular songs or going to the movies.

However, Cantonese opera has a long history of serving important social functions for its audiences both in southern China and in overseas Chinese communities, a subject I examine next.

### Cantonese Opera's Social Functions

Emerging as one of China's most important regional musical forms around the mid-19th century, Cantonese opera thrived in the Pearl River Delta area in the Kwangtung Province, which encompassed Canton and Hong Kong (Yung, 1989).[1] As popular entertainment, it reached its peak in the first half of the 20th century—a period of time when those old people mentioned earlier were young. For a long time, regional operas in China served two important social functions other than entertainment. Operatic performances, according to Bell Yung (1989):

---

[1]My discussion of Cantonese opera benefits from ongoing discussions with Bell Yung, both in person (in Pittsburgh in April, 1995) and over electronic mail, and from his book (Yung, 1989) and written review of an earlier draft of this chapter.

had always been an integral part of religious ceremonies, calendrical festivities, and rites of passage in Chinese society. . . . Secondly, the operas served for centuries as a source of information and an arbiter of moral standards and social behavior for their audiences, the majority of which were illiterate or semi-literate; *it was thus an important medium for mass communication and education.* (p. 8, italics added)

The narratives of Cantonese operas, for example, always carry such moral themes as loyalty, brevity, chastity, piety, honesty, and faithful love.

Cantonese opera performances traditionally occur in two kinds of contexts. Commercial performances take place in opera houses or rented movie theaters in urban centers before a paying and mainly middle to upper middle class audience (Yung, 1989). Ritual performances, on the other hand, often are sponsored by religious or neighborhood groups as part of religious or festival events. (This partially helps explain why Mrs. Chung and her friend sang Cantonese opera songs at their Mid-Autumn Festival street parties.) Government cultural agencies also organize these performances occasionally for the enjoyment of the people.

Ritual performances tend to take place in temporary structures, such as "giant sheds made of bamboo poles and aluminum sheets" in large open spaces (Yung, 1989, p. 37). Because the audience area in the shed is not sealed off by walls and the show is free to the public, people can and do literally walk in and out of the sheds even as the performance is in progress. Offstage activities often abound. Based on field research in Hong Kong in the early 1970s, Yung (1989) observed that:

In densely populated or easily accessible areas, with a good troupe and well-known star performers, up to 4,000 people might be present at a time . . . . In front and on either side of the big shed were food stalls and soft drink pedlars. Gambling tables and stalls, although officially not permitted, were sometimes set up around the audience area if the shed was situated in a remote area. These stalls were centers of continuous and lively activity before, after, and even during, the performances. (p. 37)

Indeed, several of Mrs. Chung's and Jennifer's friends maintained that they liked Cantonese opera because of their fond memories of going to ritual performances at a tender age.[2] "There was always so much to eat at the opera" was the first response from Lydia, a saleswoman in Chinatown. Food carts selling candies and all sorts of other snacks, including fish balls, assorted cow and pig parts stewed in gravy, and noodles, were often seen (and smelled) outside opera tents.

Angie, Lydia's friend, a cashier at a photo shop in Chinatown, had similar experiences. As a young girl in Hong Kong, Angie often accom-

---

[2]As a young boy and later a teenager in Hong Kong, in the 1960s and 1970s, respectively, I had attended several of these ritual performances in the kind of sheds that Yung (1989) described.

panied her mother to Cantonese opera performances in neighborhood playgrounds. She was always attracted to the lively activities both on and offstage. "There were always people talking [in the audience]," Angie remembered. "Neighbors, parents, a lot of them." Unable to sit still for the 3 to 4-hour performance typical of a full-length Cantonese opera, children often got up and played. Traditionally, going to the Cantonese opera—particularly in the ritual environment—was to many people as much an event for social gathering as it was an occasion to celebrate the festival or to pay respect to the deity or deities.

## Cantonese Opera in the United States

Cantonese opera also played an important social and cultural role in Chinese American immigrant communities. Ronald Riddle (1983), for example, suggested that Cantonese opera has long been an integral part of the musical culture of San Francisco's Chinatown.[3] On the East Coast, Jing Chi Kwok (1985) spoke of the existence of five Cantonese opera theaters in New York's Chinatown in its earlier years. In the 1890s, there were Tai Chung Hwa on Bowery and the Chinese Theater on Doyer Street. These two theaters were said to accommodate close to 1,000 people with rows of long wooden benches. Around the 1920s, there were Lok Chin Chau, Chuk Man On (on Bowery near Grand Street), and Wing Shen (on Grand Street). Opera titles often included the all-time favorites, such as *The Butterfly Lovers, Mook Lin Saves Mother, The Story of the West Chamber, To Serve the Fatherland with Unreserved Loyalty,* and so forth.

The majority of the audiences, according to Kwok (1985), were men working in Chinese restaurants or laundries. Because Chinese women were restricted from immigrating to the United States, most of these men either were unmarried or had left their wives in China. It was because of this that Chinatown, U.S.A. had long been characterized as a "bachelor society" (Mark & Chih, 1982). As a result, Cantonese opera actresses in New York's Chinatown at that time were much more esteemed by their predominantly single male audiences and always commanded higher income than male performers.[4] In other words, not

---

[3]Riddle (1978) also gave a more concise report on music clubs and ensembles in San Francisco's Chinese community.

[4]Women were legally restricted from the opera stage in China up until the 1920s, but the restriction did not seem to apply in Chinese America. Kwok (1985) suggested that by the late 1890s, popular Cantonese opera actresses in New York City made about $1,000 monthly, one third more than their male counterparts. Riddle (1983) also suggested the role of actresses as the principal box-office attraction on the Cantonese opera scene in San Francisco's Chinatown—except that these female opera stars did not appear in significant numbers for the first time until the mid-1920s, when two Chinese opera theaters were completed.

only did Cantonese opera serve as a link between these *lou hwakiu* (old overseas Chinese) and part of their cultural past, it perhaps gave them an entertainment with a certain romantic or even sexual fantasy. It is no wonder that New York's Chinatown sustained the livelihood of these theaters and opera troupes although it was a small immigrant community with only several thousand people at the turn of the 20th century.

However, as Yung (1989) observed, the importance of Cantonese opera as a source of information and an arbiter of moral standards and social behavior has diminished in recent decades because of "the rise in the level of literacy and the flourishing of other mass media such as cinema and television" (p. 8). Indeed, Kwok (1985) pointed out that the popularity of Cantonese opera in New York's Chinatown began to decline in the 1950s, when movie theaters gradually appeared in the area. In the ensuing decades leading up to the 1990s, drastic changes in the demographic profiles and media ecology of New York's Chinese immigrant communities led to Cantonese opera's further decline.

### Socializing Through Opera Singing

Although Cantonese opera has lost its prominence as a form of mass communication for audiences in the contemporary media ecology of New York's Chinatown, it continues to perform invaluable social and cultural functions for people who engage in it as amateur performers.[5] Private amateur Cantonese opera clubs have long been important social institutions for people in China; their members tended to come from well-to-do and upper middle class backgrounds. But the aristocratic nature of private Cantonese opera clubs faded with a growing middle class. In the United States, the socioeconomic backgrounds of the membership of such clubs in immigrant communities have become more diverse than those of their predecessors in China in decades past. Such private Cantonese opera clubs in the United States offer a place for social interaction as much as they represent a context for people to indulge in the singing of opera.

Indeed, people like Mrs. Chung, Jennifer, Lydia, Angie, Mr. Hau, and dozens of others in this interpretive community came to know each other through their affiliation with one or the other of several Cantonese opera associations in Chinatown. Called *yamngok se* in Cantonese (musical

---

[5]Two recent doctoral dissertations provide detailed discussions of Chinese musical cultures in the United States. Su Zheng (1993) examined how the developments of contemporary Chinese American music culture in New York City (of which Cantonese opera has been a part) are defined or shaped by the interaction among the host country, the homelands, and the immigrant society. Wei-hua Anna Zhang (1994) analyzed how present-day musical performance activities of the Chinese communities in the San Francisco Bay area help to preserve traditional musical styles as well as to develop new Asian American musical genres.

associations), they occasionally also organize theatrical productions. Most *yamngok se* members are amateur singers, with no prior experience in singing Cantonese opera. Interestingly, some of them initially did not join their association for Cantonese opera. For instance, Jennifer went to her *yamngok se* for the first time early in the 1980s only because some of her friends were members there. "I wasn't crazy about Cantonese opera at all," recalled Jennifer. In the beginning, she went to the association only when she wanted to see her friends.

Janet, a member of another musical and theatrical association, had similar experiences. For a period of time after she came to New York in the early 1990s, Janet's most frequent contact with people other than Chinese took place on her subway commute between her office, an advertising company in Chinatown, and her family's apartment in southwest Brooklyn along Eighth Avenue, a mixed neighborhood with a growing Chinese immigrant population. Her contact with non-Chinese diminished when she decided to change to a Chinese-operated minibus service for her daily commute, for she "felt bad seeing my mom and sister waiting to pick me up at the subway station after work." Her family was worried about crime at the station. Every day Janet repeated the same routine of "work, eat, and sleep; and work, eat, and sleep" and very soon she began to feel "the person in me was feeling useless." Joining her *yamngok se* helped Janet break the everyday routine that was beginning to wear her down. It also allowed her to meet many new friends.

Similarly, Patricia joined her *yamngok se* because "there was nothing else to do" around the time she came to New York late in the 1960s. Unlike Jennifer, Janet, Lydia, Angie, and Mrs. Chung, Patricia had some prior experience with certain Chinese performing arts. She used to teach Chinese dancing in Hong Kong and later learned to play the *yeungkam* (struck zither), a Chinese musical instrument. For a while after settling in New York, she taught in a Chinese language school in Chinatown. "I've always liked Chinese culture," explained Patricia, now a typesetter at a printing company in Chinatown after being laid off by the bank where she had also worked for many years. Through ongoing participation in her *yamngok se* and practice, Patricia has become a very proficient singer of Cantonese opera songs.

Invariably, social interactions at *yamngok se* center around the singing of Cantonese opera. In one of the weekend practice sessions Mrs. Chung brought me to, there were four or five people playing music for the members. Mrs. Chung's *yamngok se* was located on the second floor of a five-story walk-up on a narrow street near Mott Street, which for many decades was the center of political power and social and economic activities in New York's Chinatown. The space occupied by the organization resembled a small, rectangular studio apartment. Most of the walls were partially covered by half-faded black-and-white and color photographs depicting the association's members in various performance activities over the past several decades. There were also several posters announcing full-length operas produced by the association, which was first established in the 1930s on Canal Street. Some of the posters dated back many years.

Against the back wall was a platform raised several inches from the floor—with a large rectangular sign announcing the name of the association running across the top of the wall. All of the larger and heavier instruments were placed on the stage, including a few drums and wood blocks (percussion instruments) and a *yeungkam*. An array of string instruments, such as the *yiwu* (a primary instrument in Cantonese opera), were hung on the walls on both sides of the stage. Next to the stage was a wooden shrine the size of a wardrobe, where a statue of *Hwa Kwong* (patron deity of Cantonese opera) was accompanied by several burning incense sticks and fruits.

Over the years, the several Cantonese opera clubs have presented full-length operas, but the majority of their membership's performances are what Yung (1989) called "non-theatrical" or "non-dramatic" performances (p. 39). These performances do not involve any staging, costumes, makeup, choreography, sets, or props. They are, simply put, the singing of Cantonese operatic songs. Members always bring the music sheets for the songs they have prepared. The singers give out copies of the music to the musicians and the *sifu* (or master teacher) as they ready themselves for practice. Although the *sifu* supervises practice, the musicians also coordinate closely with the performer. On many occasions, when the *sifu* was not present, I observed that the lead musician, who played the *yiwu,* stopped the music and discussed with the singer areas that required improvement. Once in a while, other musicians also interjected their suggestions. At various points during the evening, a few of the members, after their singing practice had concluded, picked up their instruments to play for others. Interactions among the members, even when mistakes were being discussed, were always very friendly and cooperative.

Not only do members constantly maintain a give-and-take attitude when they are practicing, they also join together to help sustain their *yamngok se* on other occasions. All of the *yamngok se* in New York's Chinatown today are nonprofit organizations. The operating budgets of the majority of these organizations rely mainly on membership fees, donations, and income earned by performing at ritual or social events. Members volunteer their time to perform at such events as festival celebrations organized by local civic associations, weddings, and galas. To help celebrate the 1995 Chinese New Year, for instance, Mrs. Chung and many colleagues from several *yamngok se* performed *yutkuk* to about 500 people in the auditorium of the Chinese Consolidated Benevolent Association, which sponsored the event.

In short, Cantonese opera has served important social and cultural functions in southern China, Hong Kong, and many overseas Chinese communities, including San Francisco and New York City. Cantonese musical and theatrical associations in New York City serve as a ground for the adoption of karaoke. As karaoke spread within the Chinese American communities beginning in the early 1990s, the demand for *yamngok se*'s live musical service at social events began to drop. According to several members of this interpretive community, many potential sponsors shifted to karaoke. The challenge that karaoke has brought before the *yamngok se* communities in New York's Chinatown offers a rare opportunity for analyzing the uneasy yet dynamic interaction between two seemingly incompatible cultural practices. In the next section, I examine how the singing of Cantonese opera songs has been transformed in karaoke and the implications of such a transformation.

## AN OLD CULTURAL FORM IN A NEW MEDIA ENVIRONMENT

At first glance, Cantonese opera and karaoke do seem an odd couple. *Yutkuk* has long been regarded as a regional musical genre and entertainment, and a traditional way of life with over a century of history. Karaoke, on the other hand, is a new entertainment form often associated with modern technology in smoke-filled bars and noisy restaurants around the world, and is a fad in the eyes of many. In fact, of all the people in this interpretive community with whom I have spoken, none equates singing *yutkuk* with musicians and singing *yutkuk* in karaoke. Yet the two cross paths in the experience of the people in this community. How *yutkuk* and karaoke mix together presents an interesting case study of how an old cultural form is translated into a new medium and the implications of such a translation.

### Translating *Yutkuk* Into Karaoke

According to Yung (1989), the tunes of Cantonese opera are grouped into three categories. The first category is *bongwong* (aria types). The second category includes *siukuk* and *paaiji* (fixed tunes). The third category is *syutcheung* (narrative songs). About 90% of all vocal music in Cantonese opera belong to *bongwong* and *siukuk*. Yung (1989) further suggested that:

> *Bongwong* songs are important from the musicological point of view because of their structural features and how they are performed and transmitted. One characteristic is that *bongwong* tunes, when sung to different sets of text, almost always have distinctly different melodic contours; versions of the same "tune" may sound quite different from one another. (p. 67)

There are only about 30 aria types in Cantonese opera.

In contrast, *siukuk* (also known as small songs) are based on pre-existing tunes, each one of which is identified by a title (Yung, 1989). There are several hundred fixed tunes in the Cantonese opera repertoire. Through a process called *tinchi* (or, to fill in with text), *tinchi yan* (writers who *tinchi*) compose new songs by placing new texts into pre-existing tunes. The linguistic tone of the texts or the pitch property of spoken syllables is always carefully written to match the existing tunes chosen. The individual melodic contour of each of the pre-existing tunes does not vary much from version to version. Therefore, it is not difficult to conceive that singers who have mastered one pre-existing tune can sing an infinite number of songs based on this specific tune, as long as they remember the new texts.

People who like to sing Cantonese opera songs, including Mrs. Chung, Patricia, and many friends at their *yamngok se,* invariably find *bongwong* much more challenging than *siukuk*. Singing *bongwong* songs with the variety of melodic contours that they demand is, in and of itself, a creative process. It takes a tremendous amount of training, musical skill, and ingenuity on the part of the singers. Singing *bongwong* songs allows the singers more freedom to establish their musical individuality, or signature. Moreover, the performance of *bongwong* relies on close coordination between the singers and their musicians—a form of coordination and mutual support that cannot exist when people are singing with karaoke. How well *bongwong* songs are performed often depends on how well the musicians can support and collaborate with the singer on a moment-by-moment basis.[6] Although *bongwong* songs are more difficult to sing and to master, Patricia suggested they are "also more fun to do."

By nature of its material fixity, however, karaoke software simply cannot reproduce the musical versatility that live musicians can offer. This is the reason why, as Mrs. Chung and her colleagues explained to me, all of the Cantonese opera songs available in karaoke are of the fixed tune, *siukuk* variety—a fact that they acknowledged as inherently a weakness of *yutkuk* karaoke. But the fact that *bongwong* songs do not exist in karaoke form does not seem to bother most karaoke users, or casual *yutkuk* singers. Those who occasionally sing Cantonese opera songs without any training are certainly not as musically demanding or perceptive as those who are trained to sing and appreciate this type of song.[7]

---

[6]See Sau Yan Chan (1991) for an insightful study of the role of improvisation in the creative process of Cantonese opera music.

[7]It is important to note that *yutkuk* is not familiar only to trained enthusiasts. The 1960s saw a large number of Cantonese opera movies being made in Hong Kong (Yung, 1989).

Marketing considerations have also made karaoke *yutkuk* more accessible to the amateur singers. To broaden their products' appeal, karaoke developers produce relatively easy songs for the mass consumers to sing.[8] The karaoke version of music is often several keys lower than the original in order to accommodate consumers who have a limited range; this is a fact that people in this interpretive community repeatedly pointed out as they discussed some of the differences between the original *siukuk* songs and their karaoke versions. Similarly, all recent karaoke laserdisc machines have a built-in mechanism with which the users can manipulate the key of any music to their taste or competence.

Furthermore, some Cantonese karaoke laserdiscs actually mix *siukuk* songs with other Cantonese popular songs. According to Chi Hwa Wong (1990), some of the well-known, indigenous Cantonese songs in Hong Kong actually evolved from the *siukuk* genre, such as "Tears of the Red Candle," "The Red Bean Poem," and "Lotus' Fragrance" (p. 51). This helps explain why some people do not find singing *yutkuk* in karaoke problematic.

### The Shift to Karaoke

One of the reasons some former sponsors in New York's Chinatown have shifted to karaoke is the fact that karaoke offers a greater variety of musical genres than any group of musicians can offer. There can be little doubt that those people who want to sing, listen to, or do both to Cantonese opera songs will focus their attention on *yutkuk,* either with live music or in karaoke. But for those in the audience whose interest or competence is not in *yutkuk,* karaoke gives them many more choices.

Moreover, because *yamngok se* musicians appear with their fellow members as a team, they only accompany their members. The musicians from Patricia's *yamngok se,* for example, only play for their own members at events.[9] Therefore, the majority of the people in the audience would not have any involvement in the performance to speak of.

Economics is an equally important reason why some people, especially those who would have otherwise hired musicians for their social

---

Wide release of commercial recordings of *yutkuk* and radio airtime in the 1960s and 1970s made scores of *siukuk* songs familiar to many people in Hong Kong and overseas Cantonese communities. Television reruns of these movies and a great variety of *yutkuk* marketed in the form of prerecorded audiocassette tapes have performed similar functions in subsequent years. Mass-manufactured *yutkuk* products are not an obscure part of the Cantonese-language popular culture markets.

[8]Ogawa (1993b) observed that producers in Japan have created a subgenre of pop music in karaoke form meant for amateur singing.

[9]In addition to karaoke, however, a large Chinese restaurant in New York's Chinatown offers live Cantonese opera music to its customers one evening every week as a special attraction.

events, have made the shift from live music to karaoke. Because most restaurants in Chinatown nowadays offer their in-house karaoke system to customers as a complimentary service, using karaoke is much cheaper than hiring a group of four or five musicians. As discussed in chapter 1, wanting to cut musician-related costs at drinking establishments partly motivated the initial development of karaoke in Kobe, Japan, as well.

However, although karaoke has had a negative financial impact on *yamngok se,* people in this interpretive community do not necessarily hold karaoke in contempt. Some of them actually accept karaoke as part of their social, as well as their musical, lives. Occasionally, Mrs. Chung and her friends get together at parties to sing karaoke *yutkuk.* But their engagement with karaoke as an alternative form has had some unforeseen impacts on the musical experience of *yamngok se* members. In the following section, I analyze how the shift from live music to karaoke can influence the musical competence of *yutkuk* singers.

**Karaoke as an Alternative Experience**

As with any other fine or performing art, to become a proficient singer of Cantonese opera song requires a program of persistent and diligent practice. But people in this interpretive community do not get to practice in their *yamngok se* as much as they would wish. Because most of them work during the day, they can only meet for practice during the weekend. When extra practice is needed, as in preparation for a performance, they have to make an extra effort to arrange meetings at the association after work on weeknights. In addition, members also have to coordinate with the schedule of the musicians. Everyday personal, family, and business matters can always interfere with one's practice schedule. Therefore, those who long for the opportunity to sing or practice at their *yamngok se,* while having to contend with the restrictions imposed by their personal and work schedule, will always be frustrated or will have to look for alternatives. Under these conditions, karaoke has become a logical alternative for people in this community, especially when they cannot make it to their *yamngok se.*

However, for certain *yutkuk* enthusiasts, using karaoke to sing Cantonese opera pieces can have a negative impact on the singers. Several people told me that the range of some of their friends' voices in this community had become flat after they began to sing *yutkuk* more with karaoke and less with musicians. They attributed this to the more limited range and the level of key of karaoke *yutkuk* as compared to live music—a difference noted already. Those who are used to karaoke *yutkuk* are said to have developed a limited vocal range, thus making it much more difficult for them to adjust to such musical demands in live performances as transposition—the shifting from one key to another. A *yamngok se* member was reported to have lost the range she used to have after a long absence from practicing with live music, instead immersing herself in karaoke. On one occasion, this member was said to have to excuse herself from a live performance shortly after the music began, presumably because her limited range and lack of practice had failed her.

This does not seem to have stopped some *yutkuk* enthusiasts from adopting karaoke as an alternative to live music, however. Every now and then, for instance, a few of Mrs. Chung's friends go to the small and mostly unfurnished storage basement of her shop, sometimes in the middle of the day. What these people are looking for is Mrs. Chung's collection of *yutkuk* videotapes that she copied from karaoke laserdiscs and the small 13-inch color television set that has a built-in VCR. The set is connected to a sound and microphone mixer, the one that Mrs. Chung used at her Mid-Autumn Festival neighborhood karaoke parties.

Mrs. Chung's friends usually set up the system for themselves (while she conducted her business upstairs), sang for about half an hour or an hour, and when they were done, put everything back and returned to work. Oftentimes, these people came alone. "I guess sometimes they got frustrated at work and wanted some release," Mrs. Chung explained with a smile on her face, hinting at a kind of quick fix with karaoke *yutkuk*. "But I think some of them really missed it [*yutkuk*] at the time." These people literally punctuated their work day with karaoke *yutkuk*.

Although karaoke as a musical source is not as flexible as live musicians, people in this community nonetheless use it to extend their musical as well as their social space beyond the walls of their *yamngok se*. After all, despite the fact that karaoke does not include *bongwong* songs, it does give *yutkuk* enthusiasts full musical accompaniment for a growing number of *siukuk* numbers. Moreover, all of the karaoke laserdiscs that feature *yutkuk* music invariably contain matching Cantonese opera video sequences. Some of these videos are actual excerpts from Cantonese opera movies, complete with well-known actors and actresses in period costumes and stage makeup, and often dance in mesmerizing operatic choreography, all of which adds striking visual reference to the songs.

Singing *yutkuk* with karaoke has become a common feature of Mrs. Chung's and many of her friends' social lives. Oftentimes, when Mrs. Chung, Mr. Hau, Patricia, Angie, Lydia, and their friends gathered together at parties, they sang karaoke *siukuk* as the main attraction. At times, it was not uncommon for them to also sing popular songs, although it should be noted that I have never seen any of them sing any English-language song; it is clear that their main interest is in Cantonese songs. Mrs. Chung used to invite a few musicians to the shop to play Cantonese opera music. When musicians were not available, she simply used karaoke for the occasion.

In 1992, the year before she had her first karaoke neighborhood party, Mrs. Chung had her first ever Mid-Autumn Festival party with a few musicians from the *yamngok se*. But in 1993, she decided to shift to karaoke after most of her musicians were unavailable. "The musicians volunteered to help me out last year," Mrs. Chung explained. "But they don't always have time for you." For the 1994 neighborhood party, Mrs. Chung did not even bother to ask her musician friends. She just organized the event with karaoke in mind.

In short, the translation of *yutkuk* into the karaoke form has facilitated some interesting—and unforeseen—musicological, economic, musical, and social consequences. The relative material fixity of karaoke software can only accommodate *siukuk,* or fixed tunes, thereby excluding *bongwong,* the more demanding and challenging aria types in Cantonese opera. By being an alternative musical source, karaoke is a mass-produced medium and, by extension, a media industry that takes away employment opportunities from traditional opera musicians. As a result, this economic displacement has negatively impacted on the subsistence of Cantonese opera as a social institution. While karaoke proves to be a convenient alternative to having musicians for live music, it can also have limiting effects on the musical competence and development of *yutkuk* singers. Nevertheless, karaoke does allow people in this interpretive community to extend their social space beyond the walls of their *yamngok se*.

Indeed, it was through the imaginative use of karaoke that Mrs. Chung and her friends in this community were able to keep part of a tradition alive for some of their compatriots in New York's Chinatown. Interestingly, by engaging and presenting a traditional cultural practice in a new media form, people in this interpretive community also helped transform that cultural practice. In the following section, I return to Mrs. Chung's karaoke *yutkuk* party for the 1993 Mid-Autumn Festival. At the party, the tradition of singing Cantonese opera songs in the ritual mode was transformed in a unique context in the contemporary Chinese diaspora. The analysis focuses on the extent to which people can improvise on their social roles in a situation not customarily or entirely familiar to the participants.

## AN INDIGENIZED CULTURAL PRODUCTION

It is difficult to characterize Mrs. Chung's Mid-Autumn Festival karaoke parties as being the same as any traditional ritual performance of *yutkuk*. It is true that, as I demonstrate later, Mrs. Chung's karaoke *yutkuk* parties somehow remind one of certain aspects of the ritualized Cantonese opera performance analyzed earlier: the respect for traditions, the opera songs, the loose dramaturgical frame of the scene, the casual interactions among the audience members, and so forth. But the parallel between the typical ritual performance of Cantonese opera and Mrs. Chung's karaoke *yutkuk* parties is incomplete at best. At the theatrical—and most obvious—level, Mrs. Chung's karaoke scenes simply do not have such dramatic elements as the operatic plot, costumes, choreography, and live music that are intrinsic to any Cantonese opera performance.

Indeed, Mrs. Chung never made such a claim. She and people in her community never attempted to reproduce in their street parties the typical ritual performance of Cantonese opera—the regional theatrical art form that once attracted thousands upon thousands of enthusiasts in the Pearl River Delta in Kwangtung Province, China, in the mid-19th century when its popularity was at its peak. Nor did they ever try to recapture the glamour that Cantonese opera once had in Hong Kong a few decades ago, when Mrs. Chung and many of her friends from their *yamngok se* were first exposed to the art and ritual form. All that they wanted to do, instead, was to help keep part of a tradition alive. They wanted to give people in the Chinatown immigrant community, particularly the elderly (*louyanga*), some familiar entertainment in the context of a commonly occurring festival.

Karaoke as a cultural practice and the contemporary diasporic context together have helped redefine how *yutkuk* is presented and experienced in Mrs. Chung's Mid-Autumn Festival parties. If culture is indeed context, as Geertz (1973) suggested, then Mrs. Chung's Mid-Autumn Festival party in 1993 can certainly be considered a unique cultural experience. At one level of analysis, as the following section indicates, Mrs. Chung's street party offers an interesting illustration of how karaoke participants may improvise and manage their interaction with others in situations not entirely familiar to them.

Mrs. Chung's karaoke party's resemblance to a traditional street performance event might have evoked certain codes of behavior in the minds of the participants. The behavioral codes for a street performance or attendance at a street performance might have indicated what roles they were expected to play and how they might play these roles collectively in Mrs. Chung's karaoke scene. But because of the loose and not-altogether-familiar dramaturgical frame of the karaoke *yutkuk* street party, participants improvised on a real-time, in-the-moment basis in their construction and maintenance of the scene. And improvise they did.

## Karaoke *Yutkuk* Before a Roman Catholic Church

Apart from featuring *yutkuk,* what also made Mrs. Chung's 1993 karaoke street party a unique cultural experience was the fact that it took place on the sidewalk by her storefront. Instead of performing in a giant shed or a theater, as most Cantonese opera singers and audiences are accustomed to, Mrs. Chung and her friends sang *yutkuk* for their festival audience across the street from a Roman Catholic church that had a predominantly Cuban American congregation. The church is located at the southeast corner of Chinatown. Built in the Greek revival style, the church was dedicated in 1837 and scheduled to be torn down in 1986, but was eventually saved as a New York City landmark by a citizen's group spearheaded by the Ancient Order of Hibernians. Sandwiched between a grocery deli at the street corner facing a large complex of housing projects and a line of tenement buildings to its right, the church occupies about one half of its side of the street. The six cement steps, leading to three sets of heavy, tall wood doors with stained glass windows, are punctuated by several sets of bronze hand railings. The few tall stone pillars in the front of the church stand almost as tall as the building itself.

On the day of Mrs. Chung's Mid-Autumn Festival karaoke party, dozens of Chinese men and women were sitting on the church's steps watching the performance from across the narrow street. Although Mrs. Chung emphasized in her newspaper announcement that senior citizens in the neighborhood were invited, only about half of the audience were *louyanga*. Mrs. Chung thought that perhaps a slight rain in the morning had prevented more senior citizens from coming. The other half of the audience consisted of children, as well as men and women in their mid-20s to mid-40s. All of them dressed in their regular, everyday attire.

Instead of the traditional smells of candies and such indigenous Cantonese snacks as fishballs and assorted cow and pig parts stewed in gravy, the scent of coffee was in the air as Mrs. Chung and Mr. Hau carefully adjusted a large metal coffeemaker on a long table in front of a florist shop facing the church. People who walked by the store could also smell the inviting aroma of freshly baked pastries, for there were several large boxes of them sitting next to the coffeemaker. These treats were offered free to the audience, courtesy of a local bakery. Mrs. Chung had gathered other donations from restaurants, souvenir shops, and grocers in the Chinatown neighborhood. Goods or gifts donated by these small businesses were given out to the audience at a raffle at the end of the party to wish the audience good luck.

At the beginning, Mrs. Chung's son Bill and Mr. Hau were busy connecting all the wires for the karaoke sound system. Placed under a large banner with the Chinese words "Mid-Autumn Festival Celebration Neighborhood Party," the system contained a sound-mixing console connected to a few microphones on stands and two large loudspeakers facing the audience across the street. Occasionally, the loudspeakers gave out some deafening feedback screams as Bill adjusted the position of the microphones. The system was also connected to the small television/VCR set that Mrs. Chung had pulled from her shop's basement.

Another equally small television monitor was also set up facing the audience.

Because the party was truly an open event, there was no clear sense of continuity between one performance and the next. In a typical ritual performance of Cantonese opera, the flow of events onstage is dictated by a predetermined dramatic script. The flow of events in the stage area of Mrs. Chung's karaoke *yutkuk* performance was determined by an open script, one written by the spontaneous reaction of or interaction among the participants. Indeed, the order in which Mrs. Chung's performers appeared, at least from the point of view of the audience, was essentially unpredictable.

If there was indeed a flow in the event, it interestingly came from the order in which Mrs. Chung had recorded the accompaniments. Because the accompaniments were dubbed on videotapes, making it cumbersome to select and locate any specific songs, the performers mostly sang the songs in the order they were recorded on the tapes. At several points during the party, upcoming performers had to rush to the microphones in the stage area to catch up with their songs. If any performer had requested a specific song, it would have taken Mrs. Chung or Mr. Hau time to locate it. In fact, one of the longest pauses between songs lasted for more than 9 minutes, as Mrs. Chung and Mr. Hau were frantically searching for a requested song. This is an important reason why, in most other situations as long as it is affordable, people tend to use laser-based karaoke machines; they are much more flexible for music selection.

On the other hand, the interaction patterns among people appearing in the scene were quite difficult to discern. Although Mrs. Chung had acquired a temporary permit from the police to block off car traffic, pedestrians were free to roam the street. A few curious passers-by actually stopped right before an additional monitor facing the audience to watch the video as some of the performances were underway. Some time later, other passers-by literally stood beside the performers, sharing the small television/VCR set with them. Moreover, most of the people in the audience did not seem to know one another, although some of them appeared to have come in small groups, such as a few parents carrying children. There were always a few people who approached the long table to pick up tea or coffee and pastries. Those remaining on the church's doorsteps could hear one Cantonese opera song after another.

Because Mrs. Chung's karaoke scene was in an open-air public space, the aural and visual orientation of the scene also seemed somewhat chaotic at times. The music or songs were often mixed with children's laughter as the children in the audience began to play on the street. The traffic and occasional sirens from ambulances screaming by in the nearby main streets, as well as conversations in the audience and between passers-by, also made the sound environment of the scene somewhat disorienting—or lively, depending on one's perspective.

The constant crossing over of audience members between the audience area and the stage area signified the inherent dramaturgical-structural openness of the karaoke scene. The spontaneous, unpredictable, and almost volatile juxtapositions among the sights, sounds, and smells at the scene also added a conspicuous degree of sensory complexity and richness to this openness. It is true that the dramaturgical looseness and the largely unrehearsed performances by the audience members and the singers might have seemed chaotic to people outside Mrs. Chung's karaoke scene. But ironically, these were exactly the intrinsic forces—the result of human spontaneity and dramaturgical improvisation—that helped hold the scene together and give the scene its uniqueness. Looking at the scene from the inside, I noticed that all of the human and material elements directly and indirectly involved in the construction and maintenance of Mrs. Chung's karaoke scene existed in harmony.

Participants in this scene did not follow any strictly predetermined program of behaviors (Scheflen, 1964, 1965, 1979). Indeed, the ad hoc nature of the scene—that a karaoke *yutkuk* party of this kind did not have much precedent—did not give participants a definitive program to follow. To some degree, however, the faint resemblance of the scene to the typical ritual attendance and performance of Cantonese opera and street events might have given the participants a loose social frame within which they could improvise their course of actions.

It is also important to note that the technology used in the scene played an intrinsic role in the construction and maintenance of the interaction among the participants. Specifically, the fact that videotapes did not allow the participants maximum flexibility in the selection of music served to define the flow of events in the stage area and, by extension, how members in the audience reacted to these events in sequence.

This scene thus represents a synthesis of certain background knowledge of social interaction, moment-by-moment human improvisations and performances, and the imaginative use of technology in the construction and management of a unique social and cultural experience. It embodies a voice that speaks to the continuity as well as transformation of an old tradition amidst social, economic, and technological changes in the diaspora.

## A SUMMARY ANALYSIS

To the lower middle to middle-class people in this interpretive community, such as Mrs. Chung, Mr. Hau, and Patricia, karaoke serves in their everyday lives as a cultural connection to Cantonese opera singing. But this connection requires a trade-off. On the one hand, karaoke is used to foster contact with an older art form, as well as to expand the participants' social world beyond the walls of the *yamngok se* or musical associations. It also allows them to bring *yutkuk* or Cantonese opera songs to people in their ethnic community; to help keep in touch with an important, traditional form of entertainment and popular culture. Through imaginative uses, karaoke is adopted to create unique cultural experiences by combining traditional theatrical forms, new media, and cultural practices in the diaspora.

On the other hand, however, certain artistic and creative aspects of *yutkuk* singing are transformed or lost in the translation or adoption process. As Cantonese opera songs are refashioned into mass-mediated cultural products, the interactivity between the performers and musicians is lost. Moreover, an important type of *yutkuk* songs, *bongwong,* which requires sophisticated skill and coordination and is esteemed by many seasoned singers, is ignored because of the material fixity of karaoke software. The economic foundation of Cantonese opera as a social institution, particularly that of amateur, nonprofit opera associations, has also been eroded by the introduction of karaoke as mass-mediated consumer products and as a multimillion-dollar industry.

In short, the cultural practice of singing Cantonese opera songs in karaoke in this community reflects a negotiation between two media and cultural forms—two articulations of life, whereby a certain form of regional folklore, artistry, and ritual from a bygone era is being reframed and reclaimed in a contemporary, diasporic, and technological environment.

# 4

# Karaoke as Status Symbol: The Voice of a Taiwanese Community in the Affluent Suburbs of New Jersey

Unlike people in the first interpretive community in New York's Chinatown, people in the community based in New Jersey do not carry any apparent cultural baggage of having to negotiate a traditional musical form as part of their karaoke experience. Although they sing karaoke as entertainment, people in this interpretive community also engage in it as a conspicuous means to express their status, wealth, and social attainment. I begin their story in the next section by presenting an overview of this interpretive community of affluent first-generation Taiwanese immigrants in New Jersey through a karaoke scene that characterizes a part of these people's lifestyle. I then analyze how members of this community use karaoke in a variety of social contexts to articulate a way of life hardly known outside their community.

## ONE BIG KARAOKE AND DANCING PARTY

My curiosity about John, Calvin, and many of their compatriots from Taiwan arose every time people told me about what they did with karaoke. John, I was told, has a karaoke ballroom at home and everyone I talked to told me about his karaoke parties. Calvin is another story. The person who first told me about him did not even know his name. Instead, my Taiwanese friend simply said she had heard of this *Maowang,* or Cat King, a nickname attributed to Elvis Presley in parts of the Chinese-speaking world. "He sings like *Maowang,*" she told me.

It was not until the fall of 1993 that I met these people for the first time at a large karaoke and dancing gala. The evening event was organized by a small private karaoke club in New Jersey, of which John and Calvin are two of 34 members. All the guests were friends of the members or friends of their friends, each of whom bought a ticket for $10 to cover the operating cost of the gala.[1] At the gala, all club members, and some of the guests, sang karaoke songs onstage and, when they were not singing, danced to the songs that others performed.

The karaoke club had its first few galas at a small nightclub that catered to a mostly Chinese clientele in the Flushing area of Queens, home not only to Shea Stadium but to a rapidly increasing number of Taiwanese immigrants over the last two decades. When the karaoke club wanted to accommodate more guests, the gala was moved to a large restaurant in New Jersey, where all of the club members actually live.

More than 300 people attended the Fall 1993 gala where I first met John, Calvin, and many of their social and karaoke friends. Guests began to show up at the door at around 7 p.m. The restaurant is located in an exquisite town in New Jersey (I shall call it Gainsville), a neighborhood with no shortage of large, well-kept houses behind spacious front lawns and neatly trimmed hedges, on clean tree-lined streets. Guests entering through the front gate to the restaurant were welcomed by fragrances from the meticulously arranged garden.

Behind one of the doors to the restaurant was a reception area that led to the entrance area for the spacious ballroom, which was behind yet another door. Connecting the reception area to the ballroom was a warmly lit passageway sandwiched between a grill bar and a dining room overlooking the garden. In the midst of the air conditioning, the smell was an inviting, albeit confusing, mix of Martinis, garden salads, broiled seafood, beer, and charcoal-grilled steaks being served and consumed on both sides of the passageway.

Upon entering the grand ballroom, the site of the evening's event, guests were greeted at a makeshift reception table by representatives from the club. A blend of light music and small talk permeated the air. There were about 30 round tables in the audience area, some of which were being taken by the arriving guests. Most of the guests at the gala were in their late 30s to mid-50s, although there was also a small number of younger people. The majority of the men were dressed semiformally in jacket and tie. The women were conspicuously more fashionable, all clad in expensive party dresses.

Each of the tables was simply decorated, with a number card and a small tray of assorted candies sitting on a clean tablecloth. Resting next

---

[1]The average ticket price for the several karaoke galas that I attended is about $10 to $15. Dinner is usually not included, although some galas include a few snacks. There are exceptions, of course. The club that organized the Gainsville gala held its Fall 1994 event at a local hotel with an hors d'oeuvre and roast beef buffet and cash bar, with a ticket price of $28 per guest. The scale of this club's gala seemed escalating; another gala with a sit-down dinner was planned for May 1995 and cost $35 per guest.

to the candies were about 10 copies of the one-page, double-sided program listing a total of 66 songs and the names of their performers for the evening. The majority of these songs were in Mandarin and Taiwanese; 11 numbers in the program were old English-language pop songs, such as "The Long and Winding Road," "Flashdance," and "Blowing in the Wind."[2]

The middle of the ballroom was carved out as the dance floor and occupied about one half of the enormous floor space. On the ceiling was a splendid formation of five imposing crystal chandeliers, the largest of them hanging over the center of the dance area. A large red banner on the stage's backdrop announced the name of the club in golden Chinese calligraphy.

Next to the steps leading to the right side of the stage was the control center. There the master of ceremonies, after introductory remarks by the club's president, announced the program and introduced each performer. An assortment of karaoke equipment and video monitors was lined up on top of a column of tables. As part of the evening's rules of decorum, performers were asked to go onstage through the back of the control center and, when the performance was over, exit on the left side of the stage.

At the other end of the ballroom stood two long tables, one at each corner, where hot tea and coffee were available. "We're not here to get drunk, you see," one guest reminded me. "We Chinese people love drinking tea anyway," added another, as if the fact that alcohol was conspicuously absent from the ballroom had to be explained, although the same guests did not explain to me why no one was smoking.

John and his entourage of a few friends arrived after the evening's program had started. Slightly built, John has a mild manner and speaks in a voice that is as gentle as it is full of confidence. Like many of his contemporaries at the gala, John came to the United States from Taiwan in the late 1960s. By many standards, John represents a new breed of Chinese American immigrants. Coming from an affluent, medical family in Southern Taiwan whose father received his own medical training in Japan, John speaks fluent Mandarin, Taiwanese, English, and Japanese.

After medical school in Taiwan, John went to a hospital in Manhattan for his residency training, where he met his mentor, an Italian American doctor who was partially responsible for helping John start his medical

---

[2]Comparing several karaoke galas by three different private karaoke clubs, I noted that English-language pop songs represented between one sixth to one fifth of the program of any such gala. Almost without exception, they are older songs—such as those cited in the text—perhaps because these songs gained popularity among some of the participants while they were younger in Taiwan. Moreover, these songs are certainly more readily available in karaoke. Perhaps because of copyright consideration, the most current songs are not always available in karaoke form.

career in the United States. To realize John's economic assimilation into the U.S. mainstream, one may conceptualize him as a suburban Chinese who is economically well to do, well educated, culturally pluralistic, socially assimilable, and yet prefers to stay away from the relative complexity and rapidity of urban life. John is not alone in this category.

## A New Generation of Chinese Immigrants

Many of the people I met at this and similar karaoke galas have a lifestyle similar to John's. These people, particularly club members, came mostly from Taiwan and have been in the United States for 20 to 30 years. A few of them were born in mainland China or Hong Kong and were later assimilated into the Taiwanese culture either by marriage or over many years by residence, education, or both, in Taiwan. Many of the people in this community earned their college degrees in Taiwan before coming to the United States for graduate education; some hold PhD, MD, or MBA degrees. They are upper middle to upper class professionals working mostly for U.S. corporations or business owners. Coming from very comfortable backgrounds, many of these people have an annual income well in the six-figure range.

Although a substantial number of Taiwanese immigrants in the New York metropolitan area settle in middle-class neighborhoods in Queens, especially in the Flushing area and its vicinities (Chen, 1992), members of the private karaoke clubs and their close social friends live in exclusive suburban neighborhoods in New Jersey. These people are success, improvement, and competition driven and are conscious about their quality of life. However, although economically rooted in the mainstream and pluralistic in their cultural outlook, their close friends are Chinese of similar background. As the president of one karaoke club observed, "Frankly, there are interactions with Americans at the professional or business level. But when it comes to personal life, it is seldom that Chinese enter the social network of Americans, or vice-versa."

As entertainment, the gala was one big, fun-filled party with singing and dancing; as ethnic association, the gala was an occasion where guests could mingle with hundreds of their compatriots. It is a very rare occasion when Chinese immigrants are not standing in a crowd as a mostly silent or faceless minority. Together with the more mundane gossip, chit chat, and pleasantries, the gala was a time when people talked about their recent trips back home or, in a variety of ways, described how they had been doing since they immigrated. Some expressed their concern about the recent increasing waves of violence against Asians in the United States. A few others murmured their views on the Taiwan Independent Movement. Yet some others exchanged business cards to foster future professional connections. A couple even came to show off their blossoming daughter just enrolled in a prestigious university.

To the club members, however, the gala was more than just an occasion for fun, for being with their compatriots, for being part of "the majority," or for mutual entertainment. Although all of these goals are important, a gala of this kind has taken on another level of significance. For the members, the gala is also a forum they create for themselves to *fapiao* (present in Mandarin) their work. That is, they create or own the songs they choose to sing, in much the same way as artists present their current portfolio in an art gallery for public appreciation. The gala is a time for members to show off their skills, the result of painstaking practice during their club's monthly meetings, private music lessons, informal social gatherings, or all of these. A competitive spirit is in the air. As John put it with candor and confidence:

> Competition among the performers is there even though it's mostly sub-conscious. On the outside, it always is very polite and courteous. But there are three kinds of competition going on. The first is singing, the second is dancing, and the third is the clothes people wear, especially among the women who often dress up formally.

Indeed, a closer look at the people behind this and other similar karaoke scenes and the role of karaoke in these people's social lives reveals a cultural practice that is gaining acceptance by more and more people like John. Karaoke has gone beyond the simple function of entertainment to become an expression of one's social status in this interpretive community; this gives the community and its karaoke use a distinct identity. In the next section, I analyze the diffusion of karaoke as a cultural practice in this interpretive community, with a focus on the emergence of formally organized private karaoke clubs.

## PRIVATE KARAOKE CLUBS: WINDOWS TO CERTAIN WAYS OF LIFE

Were it not for the existence of private karaoke clubs, it would be difficult to learn how an upper class culture in Asian America has evolved around the use of karaoke as an expression of one's competitive drives, wealth, and social status. What is interesting about these private karaoke clubs is that they give us an organizational metaphor to conceive part of the webs of significance (see chap. 1) that the club members have spun for themselves. By the same token, these clubs offer a view of certain ways of life not on display in the more readily accessible public spaces of karaoke, such as bars or restaurants.

It is difficult to estimate the actual number of private karaoke clubs in the New York–New Jersey metropolitan area. Members from several clubs estimate that there are somewhere between 6 and 10, if not more, such clubs in New Jersey alone. Because of the private nature of these clubs, the majority of them do not have any formal organizational connection to, or even knowledge of, one another, although those members who are aware of them can and do participate in the others' galas as guests. By nature, membership in these clubs is limited to personal friends of like background. Despite the fact that many people belonging to these clubs met each other in the United States, some friendships go back to college days in Taiwan. These clubs may be characterized as part of the latest evolution of pre-existing informal social networks facilitated by the advent of karaoke. As John recalled:

> For a long while [before karaoke], after dinner, we talked about things we did as students. Later, we talked about building our career, making money. But after a while we ran out of things to talk about because we always talked about more or less the same thing. In addition, there were people who were more successful than others. In this situation, some might feel that those who were more successful were just showing off, counting money, so they stopped. Some of us like to play mahjongg. But then some of us don't play mahjongg and therefore we had little to do after dinner. At one point, we thought singing would be a good thing to do. So we started.

By implication, these people had no experience in taking turns to sing at social gatherings for mutual entertainment prior to the arrival of karaoke. Of course, the formation of private karaoke clubs in this community did not result from a sudden thought of singing karaoke as a social or entertainment activity. The development of karaoke clubs is documented here.

## Communities Transformed: The Diffusion of Karaoke

Indeed, not too many people in the New York–New Jersey area were aware of karaoke in the early 1980s. John's first experience with karaoke gives us a glimpse of how karaoke might have diffused into the New York–New Jersey metropolitan area at the time. John saw karaoke for the first time in 1983 or 1984, quite accidentally, as he put it, while visiting a Japanese neighbor. His neighbor, an advertising executive, traveled back to Japan on business several times a year and very often brought back Japanese karaoke audiotapes for home entertainment. At a party, the wife of the Japanese executive entertained her guests by playing some audiotapes. John was curious to know who the singer was and was surprised to find out that the voice on the tapes belonged to his Japanese friend and not any star.

Although John never received any formal professional training in singing, as he admitted, he always liked to sing. Like some of his longtime friends, John sang with a chorus in high school. Over weekends, he and his equally affluent friends often gathered around their hi-fi stereo systems, very much a luxury item in Taiwan at the time. Soon after his initial exposure to karaoke in New Jersey, John acquired an audiocassette system with built-in karaoke functions that he proudly proclaimed were even better than his Japanese friend's. At the time, the audio karaoke systems that John, his Japanese friends, and perhaps a few others in the area possessed, in John's subtly proud words, "were not seen in the larger American society."

Toward the end of the 1980s, many of John's friends, and dozens of others I interviewed, also came into contact with karaoke. Some of them saw it for the first time at John's parties. Others came into contact with it through friends who brought karaoke machines back from Taiwan, where karaoke as a form of entertainment was becoming popular. All the while, karaoke machines and music began to appear in a few Chinese-run music and electronics stores in New York's Chinatown and in Flushing, Queens. Through the early 1990s, the networks of Taiwanese immigrants in New Jersey who were touched by karaoke began to expand.

It is difficult, if not impossible, to estimate how many Taiwanese immigrants in New Jersey have a karaoke system at home, but ownership of karaoke machines seems extremely widespread among members of the private karaoke clubs I studied and their networks of social friends. The experience of Nancy, a manager at a large financial firm and a member of one such club, is not uncommon among her peers:

> Everybody [I know] has it. Now it's like you can't have friends or you can be out of the loop if you don't have karaoke at home. [Through karaoke, we've come to know] at least 50 families. All of them in New Jersey. Nowadays, you go to a friend's house, there's nothing to do if you don't have karaoke, especially if you don't play mahjongg.

John offered a similar, if somewhat poignant, observation:

> At this point, one has to have a karaoke machine to have friends over. *People ask you if you have karaoke when you invite them over for dinner or social gathering.* All our friends have karaoke at home. Nowadays many bring their own discs with them to dinner or a gathering. (italics added)

Karaoke has thus become a social necessity among particular groups of friends. The experiences of Nancy, John, and many others like them suggest that this community of karaoke enthusiasts is expanding at a fast pace.

Most private karaoke clubs in New Jersey meet on the average of once a month. Each member family takes a turn hosting the gathering. Upon arrival, a member signs in and in due time all members take a turn singing according to the sign-in order. At a 20-member gathering, each participant will have to wait for an hour or more for one song. Avoiding a longer wait is one reason the size of club membership is deliberately limited. With a dinner excursion to a local restaurant and some breaks for snacks and drinks, each member usually gets to sing about five to seven songs at one meeting before it adjourns at about midnight, after 8 or 9 hours. One of the private karaoke clubs has 100 members—50 married couples—so it has to rent the auditorium of a local high school for its monthly meeting. Because the schedule cannot accommodate the entire membership, only a select group of members sing at any of this club's gatherings.

Members of certain clubs take their monthly meetings very seriously, to the extent that they are rather rigid about what will be considered a proper agenda. Several club members have expressed to me their displeasure at other members. One of the more frequent complaints I have heard is that certain members do not take karaoke or the meeting seriously enough. "Karaoke doesn't seem to be their first priority," protested one club member. "These people allow their mahjongg schedule to supersede our monthly meeting schedule!"

Another kind of complaint involves disruptive behaviors at gatherings, including such karaoke decorum violation as talking while a member is singing. At one time during my research, a few discontented members considered splitting up their club just to get rid of those with other agendas.

The emergence of private karaoke clubs gives us an opportunity to examine the diffusion of karaoke as a cultural practice and, to a certain extent, the corporate managerial mannerism expressed in the organization of these clubs. On the one hand, karaoke as a cultural practice has been adopted in this interpretive community by pre-existing friendship groups. On the other hand, the presence and adoption of karaoke in these groups has helped transform the ways that members maintain or manage their interactions and relationships. Indeed, the formal club structure did not exist among most of the people in this interpretive community before the arrival of karaoke. Moreover, as I analyze in the next section, the organizational principles of these clubs embody not only a degree of goal-oriented, corporate rigidity; they also reveal a deeper sociomoral worldview of the people who are the architects of these clubs.

## THE MANIFESTATION OF A SOCIOMORAL ORDER

Some of the private clubs in this interpretive community have a well-defined organizational structure. A member of one club showed me his club's organizational chart. On it, there is a listing of all the official positions and the respective office holders, as well as a set of regulations and codes of decorum to be observed. One of the regulations indicates that no unmarried person is allowed to join the club. Why married couples only? "People at our age tend to be married," explained Louis, an executive at an international trade company who has a few children in college. "Besides, we wouldn't have time for this if we were still building a career and raising a family."

## Marriage and Membership

Louis' explanation certainly has a great deal of truth, but why is marriage a requirement if people in that age group in the community already tend to be married? Indeed, there is another concern less obvious than the one provided by Louis. Nancy revealed an interesting insight into this other concern:

> We heard people say that members are required to bring their spouse to join. They don't like married people coming alone; that can create family problems. You see, you have to put in your feeling if you want to sing well. Over time, if your wife isn't with you, you may have to transfer your emotion to someone else. It was told that something like that happened with some club that has dancing as part of their activities. Someone, as it was rumored, didn't bring his wife along. Eventually he got involved with another woman over these social gatherings.

There is a norm in the club culture that no spouse is supposed to be left out of any club-sponsored event. If a husband sings, it is preferable that his wife also sing, or vice-versa. This norm is symptomatic of the sociomoral universe of people belonging to these private karaoke clubs; it reflects a dominant presumption or ideology supporting the traditional family structure.

Interestingly, Nancy was not the only person to tell me about this alleged affair. Indeed, the affair seems to be an urban folk tale widely shared among many people in this community. Several people from different clubs told me the story at one point or another, usually in thinly disguised contempt suggesting that "It's not something I would do." I do not know if it is possible to authenticate the story, nor is it really important to do so. What is important, however, is that the story discloses certain fundamental aspects of the moral worldview of the people in the clubs.

To the extent that the story of the affair can serve as a moral metaphor, it speaks to a pre-existing sociomoral order governing the behavior of the married men and women in these clubs. It also exposes the community members' attempt to protect the social institution of marriage from any possible disruption that participating in karaoke may engender. Embedded in the story of the affair is a fear among people in this culture toward misguided feelings, emotions, and perhaps sexual drives. Although it is necessary for the performers to have a certain degree of emotional investment in their karaoke performance, as Nancy's narrative of the affair suggests, it is taboo for the emotion to go unchecked.

The experience of Calvin (*Maowang*) illustrates this point in some detail. When John's club decided to recruit Calvin, a top-level manager at a chemical company, existing members made sure that his wife, Candice, would also join. By her own admission, Candice could not sing at the time. One major reason the club wanted to recruit Calvin was the fact that he is an accomplished amateur singer whose musical skills apparently could bring prestige and heightened enjoyment to other members. Although Candice later learned how to sing quite well, both by taking singing lessons and with help from Calvin, she had some hard times in her initial participation in the club's events. During a dinner at her residence, Candice revealed to me what she partly had to go through in establishing membership in the club:

> The first time I sang I was afraid. I was shaking. I couldn't even talk after I sang. Now, I can say something after performing a song. The first time I performed at the club's event, I didn't know what I was singing. Now I can even dance a little. I think this can be nurtured through practice.

Practice she did. Candice has also gotten to enjoy her own performance now, and she and Calvin are among the favorite members in the club scene, but not without the initial sacrifices that she had to endure.

## Managed Romance

Singing songs made famous by Elvis has been both a passion and expertise that Calvin developed ever since he first saw Elvis' *Jailhouse Rock* while still in high school. At the time, Calvin was the lead singer in a band of affluent students in Taiwan. He continued to play his music after entering college, but the pace slowed down considerably because there was "too much to do in college." However, his passion for Elvis' music never subsided. After he settled in New Jersey with his family in the 1970s, Calvin spent time experimenting with homemade accompaniments by mixing and remixing his own music on open-reel tapes, without realizing the existence of mass-produced karaoke software. Calvin's eventual discovery of karaoke early in the 1990s simply thrilled him.

At the karaoke singing and dancing gala in Gainsville organized by his club, Calvin sang "Blue Hawaii" as part of the regular program. He later sang "The Hawaiian Wedding Song" and "One Night" for an encore performance at the end of the evening. The sight and sound of a middle-aged, bespectacled Chinese American chemical company executive singing and swinging like Elvis was at once a remarkable and memorable experience, not the least because Calvin did give the audience a truly enjoyable performance.

What was equally remarkable was the fact that several women in the audience, apparently at the suggestion of certain club members, volunteered to go onstage with Calvin to become what some at the scene called "the dancing girls." There were even Hawaiian leis prepared in advance for the performance. These women included Candice, a member's daughter, a guest, and the wives of several member friends. They were all up there to have some fun while helping to construct the episode.[3] As Calvin was belting out his Elvis favorites, these women were dancing either in the background or at Calvin's side. Once in a while, a couple of them would make some flirtatious gestures—throwing kisses, for instance—as if they were courting Elvis. The performances drew undivided and enthusiastic attention from the audience. The guests on the dance floor stopped dancing; some of them even walked to the front to give their applause. Appreciative laughter and a few catcalls from some guests fought for attention in the midst of the music and excitement on and off the stage.

In the context of the karaoke club, Calvin can be said to have two identities. On the one hand, he is a loving husband, a devoted father of two college graduates, and a hard-working professional in his field. He is always so low-key that, during our conversations in his quiet empty nest on a spacious and tranquil New Jersey street, I often had to ask him to raise his voice just so I could hear what he was telling me. One can always see the earnestness, maturity, and caring radiating from his eyes whenever the subject of his wife or children is raised. Calvin the family man is easily a standardbearer for the sociomoral order that members of his karaoke club attempt to uphold.

On the other hand, however, Calvin takes on a different social identity and a dynamic persona while in the karaoke stage area. This public persona of Elvis seemed to have been dormant for all those years since his youthful days in Taipei and when building a family and career in New Jersey, only to be brought back to life through karaoke. In the stage area at the Gainsville gala, Calvin was the young Elvis, someone very much alive, at once playful, showy, and forever surrounded by women. He was one of the most visible personalities at the gala. Indeed, no one but Calvin was asked to give an encore performance, not even the few

---

[3]I also observed women performers, including a couple from this group of five, at this and other galas using friends of both genders as their dancers. But they are guests, and not formal members, of the clubs.

other club members whose performances were comparably strong and laudable.

However, the playfulness, youthful romanticism, and even sexuality projected onstage were carefully monitored by the watchful eyes of the wives, husbands, and parents at the scene. Interestingly, Calvin had considered outfitting the dancing girls with short Hawaiian straw skirts. He gave up on that idea partly because the skirts would have been more revealing than the women's own skirts. He was afraid that such an arrangement might go too far. As Calvin explained to me, "It involves other people's wives, you see."

In other words, people in the club are not in contempt of music that speaks to love, desire, or even playful romance. Nor do they object to any emotional investment in what they do while in the karaoke stage area. What they are wary of is the possibility that their spouse's emotional investment in the performance may be improperly channeled to someone else. There is an irony inherent in this karaoke way of life for people in this community: Emotions may run freely only as long as they are kept in check onstage or within the stage area and do not create family problems.

## THE DISPLAY OF WEALTH

This section focuses on certain objects that people in this interpretive community use, such as their karaoke facility and house, in the articulation of part of their way of life; namely, their wealth and social class. According to Leeds-Hurwitz (1993), objects that people use "signify culture by making concepts and assumptions visible" (p. 147). Of course, what Leeds-Hurwitz referred to are not just objects in and of themselves, but the meanings or symbolism that people attach to the objects they use and display in the construction of their social worlds. Indeed, what people in this interpretive community employ in constructing the social spaces for their karaoke activities, as I demonstrate next, serves to express their wealth and social class.

As karaoke singing is the main attraction of most social gatherings in this community, it is important for the hosts to have the appropriate facility to entertain their guests with. A complete hi-fi system with a laserdisc karaoke machine is the standard equipment at present in this community. Without exceptions, the hosts always treat their guests generously, providing ample snacks and beverages. "Playing with these things isn't cheap," a club member once admitted. "To get things set up will cost a couple of thousand dollars [at the minimum] and that doesn't include [karaoke laser] discs. So, one has to spend some money to keep up."

There are at least two levels to understanding what this club member meant by "to keep up." At one level, the players have to keep up with the hardware, software, or music collections available on the market. At another level, they have to keep up with what the other players in the community have. At this second level of keeping up, a much more subtle competition among some members in this community becomes apparent. Another club member once conceded, "A member's family economic background can be an issue. Some members are wealthier than others. There is this kind of comparison, like whose place is bigger." At this level of comparison and competition, the offering of up-to-date karaoke facilities or generous treatment of guests is not only an expression of social grace and friendship, it also is a vehicle for the display of one's personal wealth and social class.

## A Private Karaoke Ballroom

Of all the private karaoke spaces I have been to, nothing can compare to what John exhibits in his house. The French provincial chateau that John built for himself, his wife Vivian, and their teenage daughter early in the 1990s occupies about 6,500 to 7,000 square feet of space on a half-acre of land. Of course, John is not alone among his friends and neighbors in having such a large house. In fact, someone in the community characterized John's house as being small compared to the house of another medical professional who belonged to another club. But what John has in his 4,000-square-foot basement certainly was peerless, at least at the time of my visits in 1993. One half of the basement contains John's very large study and a general recreation area. In it, there are two mahjongg tables, a pool table, an arcade-style video game machine, a bar, and a full bath. The second half of the basement is the real gem: a 2,000-square-foot karaoke ballroom.

The interior of the ballroom is lit, with recessed lights in the ceiling and light fixtures elsewhere to provide a conspicuous sense of coziness. It is acoustically designed, with numerous speakers installed at the top of the two long walls to beam sound to the solid wood dance floor at a 45-degree angle. One of the long walls is adorned by tall, mirrored panels that reflect the moving images of people entering or dancing in the ballroom. Part of the ceiling is also covered with mirrors to give people a view of the dance floor and themselves at an angle; the mirrors also reflect light from the mirrored ball hanging from the ceiling.

On the other side of the ballroom are the two entrances. Between the two entrances, the Chinese word *wu* (dance) is carved into a wood panel on the wall. Besides its calligraphic elegance, this artifact does not seem to have added much to the space except, perhaps, for the symbolic redundancy or excess connoted by its very presence. After all, no guest is likely to enter the ballroom without being first informed of its purpose by the hosts.

At one end of the ballroom is a stage equipped with a large-screen, front-projection television system. On the left side of the stage is a wall full of audio and video equipment of every conceivable variety. At the back of the equipment bank is a room for wiring the network. John designed the flow chart and did the patching for the entire audio-video system, as he once told me with subtly disguised pride. The system is equipped with a video camera to record performers. A substantial number of karaoke laserdiscs are stored next to the equipment bank ("I don't really know how many I have"). A custom-made catalog describing the selections is always handy for the guests. The wall on the other side of the stage is covered by hundreds upon hundreds of audiotapes and videotapes, including some audiotapes John made of himself ("I sometimes listen to my singing in the car to see what I can improve upon"). At the front edge of the stage are two small video monitors resting on a three-foot stand to show the performers the karaoke video they are singing to.

Directly across the long dance floor from the stage is another mirrored wall. On it, there are a pair of large and vividly-carved dragons painted in stunning gold. The bulging eyes and fierce claws of the two dragons converge on a pearl. The artifact is an iconographic representation of a Chinese aphorism "*shuang lung cheng chu*" ("two dragons fighting for a pearl"). In Chinese mythology and literature, the icon of the dragon connotes the imperial, the noble, the talented, the powerful, or the fearsome; it symbolizes the male as well. The pearl, at first glance, may simply mean something precious, as in jewelry. In the context of the saying, however, the pearl actually symbolizes a woman.

At one level, this icon can be regarded simply as a decoration, for its visual form does denote a conspicuous sense of rhythm that is supposed to exist in this carefully engineered and appointed space. At the connotative level, however, the artifact suggests a degree of self-reference—of supremacy, competitiveness, and wealth. In the context of John's karaoke ballroom and the lifestyle it belongs to, the icon seems to suggest the conspicuous grace and force in the men's pursuit of, or fight for, the woman of their choice, something precious, or, simply, something worthy of being won.

John's karaoke ballroom is the site of numerous singing and dancing parties all year long. "Sometimes once every other week," said Vivian, John's wife, a homemaker whose tender hands suggest to me a carefree and comfortable life. Although John himself should know that being in such a fanciful private karaoke space is an extraordinary experience for his guests, he and Vivian often go out of their way to please or impress them further. At one of John's parties, he and Vivian treated the 15 or so guests, a small number by their standard, to an array and quantity of snacks and beverages that was simply overwhelming. There was a great variety of candies, pastries, cakes, and fruits, including the relatively expensive *longan* ("dragon eyes"). There were snacks from Japan, including some processed dried fish bone that was as crunchy as it was mysteriously tasty. There was a steady supply of beer and soda, and Henessy cognac was served throughout the evening although none of the guests seemed to be excessive consumers of alcohol. All of these snacks and beverages were placed on long tables about 20 feet from the stage, where the guests were seated and chatting while waiting for their turn to sing.

With such a fancy karaoke ballroom at home, John has become a kind of public figure in an otherwise private social circle. A Hong Kong Cantonese lumberyard owner in the Woodside neighborhood of Queens said he heard some contractors in Flushing talking about "this Taiwanese doctor spending a lot of money on this ballroom." A Taiwanese research scientist at the Bell Labs in New Jersey, who has never seen John, also heard from his colleagues about John's karaoke ballroom and "those parties." Certain Miss Chinatown pageant winners were brought over for parties as if such visits symbolized a mutual glamorization of wealth and beauty. Once, before a party began, a guest who was being introduced to me asked, rather rhetorically I thought, "You haven't been here before?" His this-is-the-place-to-be tone of voice seemed to suggest that John's karaoke ballroom is a mecca where partakers of the good life should all pay homage. Speaking in a louder voice than necessary, he may have said this as a way not only to punctuate his surprise but also to send an indirect, public compliment to our hosts who were standing nearby.

Toward the second half of the same party, some of the guests began to take to the dance floor in pairs. Dancing is a standard feature of John's karaoke parties, as it is at all galas organized by the private clubs. In fact, ballroom dancing is an important aspect of this community's culture, and many people are proficient ballroom dancers. Along with singing and fashion, as John said earlier, dancing is an area of competition for many people in this community. The party took on a different dimension once dancing started around midnight. The participants were split into two small groups; there were those who stayed to sing and those who flew to the dance floor. There seemed to be a tacit understanding between these two groups of people: The singers picked songs that the dancers could dance to. Occasionally, a couple of singers or dancers reversed their respective rolès.

Although it was already past midnight, the ballroom was animated by the new waves of music and the dancing images both on the dance floor and from the mirrors on the wall and ceiling. Following the graceful choreography of John and Vivian waltzing toward the other end of the ballroom, the guests approached the other mirrored wall, where the dragon artwork, symbolizing power and pursuit, can be found.

In short, by focusing on John's karaoke ballroom and the scenes that occur therein, I have analyzed how karaoke-related objects and activities are used in this interpretive community as a means to display and express people's wealth and social class. To a great extent, the ballroom and the lifestyle it embodies signify the affluent material conditions in which people in this interpretive community engage karaoke as a cultural practice. The ballroom itself also reveals a certain degree of social exclusivity because people from outside would have no access to this social world and other similar karaoke spaces. This section examines how karaoke-related objects, spaces, and scenes are used to express one's wealth and social status, and the next section analyzes how private singing lessons, apart from being a way to achieve higher musical attainment, are also a means to express one's status in this interpretive community.

## PRIVATE SINGING LESSONS FOR PUBLIC PRESENTATION

As the level of musical attainment can easily attract envy, how musical competence is acquired can also be understood as an expression of one's social status in this interpretive community. With perhaps a few exceptions, many people in this community have had little or no formal musical training prior to their exposure to karaoke. As a result, and similar to many of their counterparts in Asia (Wei, 1992), an increasing number of people in this community have taken up singing lessons. As I described in the beginning of chapter 1, having to sing karaoke without any prior experience can be quite an unnerving experience. Several people confessed to me that they virtually lost their voices the first time they sang karaoke in public.

Many of these people did eventually come to feel comfortable to varying degrees with singing karaoke. As someone in this community put it, "In the beginning, you don't want the microphone to come your way, but very soon you won't want to let go of it." Of course, such comfort or self-confidence does not necessarily reflect the actual level of competence of the novice. Because the echo mechanism in the karaoke machine can make even a rough voice sound soft—a technological remedy for a perceived human inadequacy—people can literally be deceived as to how well they sing. Some positive feedback, even if it is given as a matter of courtesy, can also ease one's anxiety. However, with some experience and a degree of self-consciousness, most karaoke beginners soon come to realize their limitations. Their weaknesses become even more pronounced when they come across more difficult songs. This is one of the major reasons why taking karaoke singing lessons has become a necessity for some people.

## Learning to Sing for Improvement

There are two general types of karaoke singing classes, the *ta pan* (big classes) and the *hsiao pan* (small classes). *Ta pan* are usually organized by and held at music schools located in urban areas, such as Flushing, that also sell or lease musical instruments. These classes are open to the public and their tuition is generally moderate.

In contrast, *hsiao pan* usually refers to private lessons held at the residence of the students. All the club members I spoke to who are taking singing lessons attend only *hsiao pan*. Their music teachers are invariably Mandarin- or Taiwanese-speakers, or bilingual in these two dialects. Mandarin songs tend to be the key focus of the lessons. Each small class has 6 to 10 students, who pool tuition together for their *laoshih* (teacher) to visit them, usually about once every other week. Classes are always held in the evening because of the students' work schedules.

Similar to a club's monthly meetings, students take turns hosting their classes, and snacks and beverages are always generously provided. Unlike the typical monthly meeting, class activities are very much under the direction of the teacher and not the members. More than half of the class time is spent repetitively practicing the songs chosen by the teacher, although once in a while some students may ask their teacher to teach them songs they want to learn. Oftentimes, at the end of class, the guests may suggest that the couple hosting the class sing an extra song or two; this request is seen as a token of appreciation for the hosts' accommodation. The value of this gesture does not lie in the fact that the hosts get to sing more songs but in the goodwill of the guests to offer their audienceship.

Many people in the community who take music lessons take them very seriously. I was once denied access to a class at a member's large house in an expensive neighborhood in New Jersey. That class turned out to be the term's final examination. "Your presence may influence our performance in the exam," explained the male host, very politely but with a straight face. A top-ranking executive of a major global corporation, the host would only grant me an interview over dinner at a local Chinese restaurant before he, his wife, and their *laoshih* went home to meet their classmates for their examination. I later acquired a videotape of that session. The tape shows the students standing next to a couch, often in a group, singing very intently in the direction of the camera. The tape goes on like that for more than an hour.

## Karaoke Teacher as a Status Symbol

Having a *laoshih* seems to have become yet another status symbol in the culture of this community. In the beginning, taking singing lessons is an earnest effort to acquire some basic techniques or to improve one's skill. As one student put it, "to be able to sing better is to enjoy the experience better." True enough. But very soon, having a *laoshih* becomes more than just a way to self-improvement. At a gala that was organized by a relatively new club, I witnessed a peculiar episode where the *laoshih* of the organizers was displayed as a status symbol.

In the middle of the evening's program, as the *laoshih* was being introduced for a special performance, her club member students lined themselves up at the front of the stage area. The process of mobilizing these people literally stopped the show and riveted the attention of the 200 guests in the audience. Without a doubt, what those club members did was an act of respect to acknowledge their *laoshih*. After all, to pay respect to one's teacher is always considered proper behavior and a virtue in Chinese culture. But there was something awkward about the performance of this episode. Why wasn't the *laoshih* given the entire stage to herself for the undivided attention her singing deserved?

I suggest that, as the students were showing respect to their *laoshih*, they also were attracting visual (and therefore social) recognition from the audience. The column of more than 16 brightly, elegantly, and expensively dressed men and women simply was too much of a visual distraction for the slightly built teacher to overcome—even with the red stage dress she wore. The eyes of many in the audience were in fact busy scanning back and forth between the teacher, who sang earnestly and expertly, and her students, who at times were nodding their heads in appreciation.

This episode gave an unmistakable impression that the students—the scene's producers—wanted to be seen and recognized as much as they wanted their teacher to be seen and recognized. They put themselves on display. It was like a reciprocal compliment of sorts, in that the students gave their teacher face just as much as the teacher was positioned to give her students face. There were dual benefits to be gained. With the support of her students, who are well-connected in the community, the teacher gained prestige and recognition that would bring her more students in the future.[4] At the same time, the presence of the *laoshih*, together with her skilled performance, suggested what her students might some day achieve. As the Chinese aphorism goes, "*minshih ch'u kaotu*" ("a great master produces disciples of high quality"). The presentation of the *laoshih* in this scene seemed to have been used to connote to the audience that her students, the gala's organizers, were a class above the rest.

In short, although taking private music lessons with a *laoshih* serves an unmistakably educational purpose for people in this interpretive

---

[4]I met this teacher 1 year later at a karaoke gala, where I was told her engagement with these small classes had doubled. At this more recent event, there were at least three such *laoshih* and two dance teachers presenting special performances.

community, one's *laoshih* can also be constructed and displayed as a status symbol in certain contexts. In the next section, I return to the karaoke singing and dancing gala in Gainsville to examine how members in this interpretive community put their own performances on public display. More importantly, I analyze how the karaoke performances in this interpretive community are gauged socially.

**A WINNING PERFORMANCE**

Preparing for the karaoke singing and dancing gala (or "the big party") in Gainsville in the fall of 1993, as with all other similar galas, was a long and deliberate process for some club members. It was especially so for those devoted members who have come to regard the gala as an occasion to *fapiao* (present) their work; that is, as if their performance would be judged by a public court of jurors. Of course, no one would say explicitly that there was any kind of competition going on among the participants, as John suggested earlier. But the pressure of not doing badly or not being outdone certainly was on the minds of many club members. In speaking of the competition, Louis, the trading company executive, observed:

> To a certain extent, people like to show off. That's why this kind of large-scale singing gala is more attractive to people. People like to show off. Especially when there are a lot of people around, the extent of interest would increase . . . . Of course, you want to do very good whenever you do something. You also hope to do better than other people . . . . More or less, there is this hint of competition.

Indeed, the preparation for a winning performance at the gala begins months before the gala is to take place.

### Setting up the Show

Each club member is entitled to sing one song at the gala. Members are required to sell 10 tickets each; that is, 20 tickets for each member family. For every additional 6 to 10 tickets sold, depending on the rules of the individual club or circumstances, each member can invite a guest to sing one song. At the gala in Gainsville, for example, there were a total of 66 songs in the program. More than a third of the program was performed by members. What separates club members from invited guest performers is how their performances are placed. Very often, club members will get the slots in the middle of the program (or the evening) because, according to one theory, the majority of the audience will be present then and will be most attentive around those hours.

About a month before the event, each prospective performer is asked to submit two choices to help programmers avoid repetition. The majority of the songs chosen are to the rhythms of the tango, three-step, cha cha, waltz, or disco that the guests in the audience can dance to. All the chosen numbers are then recorded onto VHS tapes according to an order determined by the gala organizers, so the program can go on continuously without interruption. Some clubs ask their guests to bring their own discs, but the process of changing discs often interrupts the flow of the program, and can cause other problems. For example, I witnessed a brief episode (at another gala) where a guest had to withdraw from the program because she brought the wrong disc.

## Varying Qualities of Performances

The quality of the performances can vary dramatically from one performer to the next. At the Gainsville gala, John's stirring, *enka*-style Taiwanese rendition of "Why Is Spring So Cold?" certainly was one of the night's most engaging high points. Originating from Japan, *enka* refers to songs of unrequited love. Calvin's "Blue Hawaii," "The Hawaiian Wedding Song," and "One Night" were, as I analyzed earlier, show stoppers. At the other extreme, however, there were several painfully unrecognizable numbers whose singers could not seem to follow even the most basic of tunes. Many of the performers had to follow the lyrics on a monitor.

Some guests seemed quite well-prepared and were able to put more into their performance than singing (or sounding out the words) alone. A trio of young women gave an energetic song-and-dance interpretation of Irene Cara's "What a Feeling" from the movie *Flashdance*—a performance that was coordinated with both the young women's black mini-skirts and their dance movements. A male club member gave a visually stunning performance of a segment from the Peking opera "Wang Chiu-Jun," which is about a beautiful woman by that name who was forced to marry the emperor of a barbarian land in ancient times to avoid his invasion of her country. The performer wore very thick makeup and dressed himself up in a full and brightly colorful Peking opera costume. Holding a horse-whip prop, this gentleman, a former sea captain, imitated the voice and movement of Wang Chiu-Jun in operatic excess as the female character was about to leave her country on horseback.

On the other hand, there were performances by quite a few guests who knew the words to their songs but did not seem to know where to put their hands or otherwise what to do between verses. Some of them actually walked off the stage even before the music was over.

## Social Construction of Musical Approval

What was equally remarkable about the performances during the evening was how they were judged or responded to. I observed three general
types of audience response in this kind of environment. The first type is
what can be called an appreciative response, which is given to any
performance that is perceived to be musically accomplished. The second
type is obligatory response, which, in accordance with the most basic of
karaoke decorum, is the kind of civil applause an audience is inclined
to give to any performance. The third is partisan response, which is
given by the friends or supporters of the performer, regardless of the
quality of the performance as a whole.

Noticeably good or outstanding performances tended to receive more
uniformly enthusiastic, appreciative responses. As a guest at the gala
put it, "You know good music when you hear it, even if you don't have
any musical training. You just feel it. To a good performance like this,
you give your heartfelt applause." Indeed, appreciative responses were
always rewarded to those singers who gave good performances.

But many performances at the Gainsville and other similar karaoke
galas drew more or less obligatory or partisan responses, which are in
essence socially constructed gestures of good will and civility. For example, after her performance of a popular Taiwanese song about happiness,
a woman was met with exceptionally enthusiastic responses from the
audience. At first, I thought her performance was very good. Her voice
was loud and clear. The fast pace and cheerful mood of the song was
emotionally uplifting and it was entirely fitting for the occasion of the
gala.

I came to a different understanding, however, after consulting a
musicologist at my table. A native Taiwanese, the musicologist contended that the singer, a Mainlander whose primary dialect was not
Taiwanese, was unable to convey the true Taiwanese spirit of the song
because she sang with an accent. He also thought her musical performance not very accomplished either, a so-so performance. I later found out
that the singer was well-known in this community and, together with
her family, had brought a large number of the guests to the gala.

In other words, whereas appreciative applause is always given to
outstanding performers, the level of applause that performers can
garner also depends to a considerable extent on their own popularity at
the gala or in the community. The more guests a performer knows at the
gala, the more applause the performer will get, certainly an incentive
for people to sell more tickets to their friends. This helps to explain why
the applause that many of the mediocre performances receive tends to
be localized, in the sense that it often comes from the specific physical
area where the friends or supporters of the performer have congregated.

## A SUMMARY ANALYSIS

People in this interpretive community, such as John, Calvin, and Nancy, are active in the affluent suburbs of New Jersey. Unlike people in the previous community, they are not obliged to adapt an older art form to a new media ecology. Instead, they pick up karaoke in their media environment and incorporate it as part of their contemporary social life. In the process of such an incorporation or adoption, the nature of their social networks is transformed. What used to be informal interaction among friends became more formalized, in the form of private clubs, from which various organized cultures arose. The organizational structures that the clubs and galas entail are not found in the other two communities' karaoke activities. Moreover, the ways in which people in this interpretive community interact among themselves within the organization embody a sociomoral view largely consistent with the worldview of the dominant social structure. Although it is true that people in this community are good friends, doing karaoke is a not-so-subtle form of competition among them. Doing karaoke has also become a means to display their wealth and social status—through the use of various objects and self-defined spaces. For some of the people, the process and means for obtaining higher musical attainment is also used as a reminder of their status in the community, both musically and socially. At a certain level, the frame of reference that these people employ in engaging karaoke is an expression of the frame of reference that they acquire and use in their professional lives, where they have found success as first-generation immigrants in the United States. The karaoke practices in this community symbolize a certain competitive drive and the pursuit of attainment through technology.

# 5

# Karaoke as Escape: The Voice of a Malaysian Chinese Community in Flushing, New York

People from the third and final interpretive community in this study come from a social and economic class that is different from those of the first two communities. Most of the members in this interpretive community were born and raised in economically deprived families in Malaysia. Many of them are undocumented workers living in the Flushing area of Queens in New York City. For people in this interpretive community, karaoke is as much a therapeutic "heaven" as it is leisure entertainment. Through karaoke, they create for themselves dramaturgical contexts where they can temporarily escape from the humdrum routine of everyday life and an otherwise oppressive social and economic environment.

The following section introduces one of the main participants in this community, Ah Maa; it provides an overview of the social, economic, and ethnic background of other members of this interpretive community as well. As with the previous two case studies, my narrative (and analysis) of this interpretive community relies not only on people's words—their voices—but also on nonverbal components that are integral to these people's karaoke scenes and experiences.

## AH MAA AND HER BIRTHDAY PARTIES

Ah Maa turned 55 in the summer of 1993, and almost everybody she knew at the time showed up at her karaoke birthday party. In fact, she had three karaoke birthday parties that summer. The first party was paid for by Cathy—whom Ah Maa calls *kaineui* (or "adopted daughter" in Cantonese)—a painfully shy widow in her mid-30s who has three young children back in Malaysia. This party took place at a Southeast

Asian restaurant in Flushing, Queens. A week later, a few other friends gave another party at the same restaurant so that Ah Maa could thank Cathy, who could not attend the party she paid for because of a last-minute, out-of-town business obligation. As a goodwill gesture, the restaurant's owner, Timmy, a gentle middle-aged entrepreneur, threw yet another party for Ah Maa a week later, although this time it was a sit-down dinner for only about 10 guests.

The second party had the largest turnout, with a total of about 60 guests attending. Not all of the guests stayed for the whole period, but many of them did. The first few guests began to arrive when the clock approached 11 p.m. Most of the people Ah Maa knows work 6 days a week, and some of them work long hours. This is why all of the karaoke gatherings Ah Maa goes to start around midnight on Saturdays.

The restaurant is located on a side street just off Main Street in downtown Flushing. During the day, downtown Flushing is a busy hub for commuters in transit between points in Queens, Manhattan, Long Island, and even Westchester County just north of the Bronx. It is an area with a robust local economy fueled by new immigrants from around the world. Koreans, Taiwanese, and East Indians are among the largest new immigrant groups in the area (Deutsch, 1994). After the evening rush hours, however, most of Flushing's downtown area is quiet. Toward midnight, even on Saturdays, there are few people on the street.

There were not many customers in the restaurant when Ah Maa's friends began to arrive for the second party. It is a relatively small restaurant, offering a mix of Southeast Asian cuisines, including Malaysian, Thai, and Indonesian fare. Hanging on the wall in the back of the restaurant was a small statue of *Gwan Gung* (or "the War God"), accompanied by burnt incense and oranges in a small, red, wooden shrine, staring down at the dining area and the door. A popular folk symbol, the statue was placed there to protect against any evil spirit that might try to enter from the outside.[1] There were about 15 tables in the restaurant. At a table near the kitchen door, a middle-aged waiter with a half-consumed cigarette spilling smoke onto his face was leisurely stuffing pairs of chopsticks into new paper jackets for the next day's business. Another middle-aged man was going in and out of the kitchen, gathering garbage. Two other waiters were sitting at a table, either staring into space or occasionally glancing over to the few customers at another table. All the people working at the restaurant knew Ah Maa. "Just ask for Ah Maa and people will show you to the basement," Ah Maa told me when she invited me to the party.

---

[1]The statue of *Gwan Gung* is also widely used by law-enforcement agencies in Hong Kong, such as police precincts, as a symbol of protection against evil forces.

It seemed to me that someone had just washed the stairs to the basement, for there was a strong scent of ammonia in the air. Each of the guests, including me, could feel the residue of moist yet stubborn dirt while descending the steps. The fluorescent lamps overhead gave off a low hum and their pale light made people look and feel cold.

The first room, by the end of the stairs where the narrow basement corridor began, was a storage space without a door. Pasted on the wall in the back of this storage room were a few half-worn cheese-cake calendar posters of Hong Kong, Taiwan, or Southeast Asian movie actresses. Partially blocking the view of these posters were racks of restaurant supplies. There were big aluminum containers of cooking oils, numerous bags of rice, jars of pickled vegetables, and bottles upon bottles of soy, fish, and red-hot pepper sauce. It was a peculiar feeling that the sight of these sauces and pickled vegetables evoked in my mind; they reminded me of appetizing aromas and tastes, yet all I could really sense was the smell of the invisible dampness, old dirt, and leftover cigarette fumes in the basement. The visual and olfactory features of this space certainly contrasted with that of the catering restaurant in Gainsville, New Jersey, that housed the big karaoke gala by the affluent interpretive community, or that of the narrow street where Mrs. Chung had her karaoke *yutkuk* parties directly across from the Roman Catholic church.

Between the storage room and a small bathroom at the end of the corridor were the restaurant's two party rooms. Next to the bathroom was the smaller, undecorated party room, covered only with bare wood panels on the wall. A round dining table and chairs occupied the bulk of the floor space.

Ah Maa's party was held in the bigger room next door, about three times the size of the smaller room. The arriving guests could hear Ah Maa's loud and raspy laughter echoing through the hollow wood-panel door. In the middle of the room was a column of three square tables covered with white tablecloths, on which there were several bottles of soda and paper or plastic cups. About 35 to 40 unfolded chairs were lined up against three of the walls. Several 60-watt wall-mounted lamps mildly yet warmly illuminated the room. Next to the door was the wall where the television monitor was hung. The monitor overlooked the karaoke system sitting on a stereo rack on the floor. When I first arrived, a couple of guests were testing the system by tapping on the microphones and playing with the buttons on the machines. Standing just in front of the karaoke system, Ah Maa was busy greeting her guests as more and more of them were arriving. "You really give me face coming," Ah Maa repeatedly emphasized to her friends with a voice that was as joyous as it was appreciative.

## Global Migrant Workers

The majority of Ah Maa's friends are Malaysians of Chinese ancestry. Many of them are recent immigrants to the United States, mostly within the last 5 to 10 years. The Malaysian population in the United States is very small. According to the 1990 U. S. Census, only 34,000 foreign-born Malaysians were reported (U.S. Bureau of the Census, 1993, p. 50). Many of Ah Maa's friends live in the multiethnic working class neighborhood of Flushing. Many of them hold low-skilled and low-paying jobs in such places as warehouses, restaurants, lumber yards, and garment factories; some others work in offices as clerks or technical support staff. Although they often speak Cantonese among themselves, with a touch of Southeast Asian accent, people in this community are proficient in the native Malay language and a combination of several other Chinese dialects, such as Hakka, Foochow, Teochius, Hainanese, and Mandarin. Some of them have a good command of English, whereas others hardly get by at a functional level. Some of the people in this community cannot read or write standard Chinese.

Like most early Cantonese immigrants in New York's Chinatown, Ah Maa and many of her friends mostly came from humble social, educational, and economic backgrounds. At a very young age, for example, Ah Maa was taken to Malaysia by her parents from her birthplace in southern China after Japan began its invasion of China and before World War II was over. Ah Maa never had enough education to develop the ability to read or write Chinese (or any language) at a functional level, an inadequacy she now regrets enormously, in part because she cannot "read those words on the television to sing karaoke."

Since marrying her husband, "a quiet and simple man," Ah Maa has spent most of her life working menial jobs to help raise their seven children. The last long-term job she had in Malaysia was as a cleaning lady for a Japanese company in the city of Kuala Lumpur. On Saturdays she would moonlight as a *daaikamje,* a woman hired to accompany a bride on her traditional Chinese wedding day until the evening banquet is over.

One day in 1986, after speaking to friends returning from the United States, Ah Maa told her husband that she wanted to travel to America on a pleasure trip. What Ah Maa really had in mind, however, was to come to the United States to work, make "a lot of American dollars," and then "go home to live my last years with my *lougung* and my youngest daughter. Buy a house for sure." (*Lougung* is a colloquial way of addressing one's husband in Cantonese.) Ah Maa sensed that her husband knew she was actually traveling to the United States to work, but he did not make any noise about it. As Ah Maa explained to me, half-jokingly, her husband was a Malaysian *wongdai* (or emperor), which meant that he had the title of a husband but no actual power.

Not unlike many early European and Asian immigrants to the United States a century or so ago (Takaki, 1989)[2] as well as some of her Malaysian contemporaries, Ah Maa came to the United States as a migrant worker who had no intention of putting down roots in the country. Ah Maa and an undetermined number of her karaoke friends are undocumented immigrants.[3] Mostly in their mid-20s to late 30s, these people came to the United States on a visitor's visa in search of work, and simply stayed beyond their visa's expiration date. Every 5 years, when their Malaysian passports are about to expire, they return home to see their families. Some of them remain in Malaysia thereafter. Some others, especially those who have not saved enough or who want to come back, may renew their passports and return to the United States or go wherever else they may find better economic opportunities.

Ah Maa has returned to Malaysia only once since she first came to the United States in 1986. In the early 1990s, she was a housekeeper and nanny for a couple from Hong Kong. The couple were business people and had a large piece of property in an expensive neighborhood overlooking the Long Island Sound. They gave Ah Maa a small room in the house and paid her under the table, starting with $250 a week (6 days) without benefits. During the day, Ah Maa was all by herself doing household chores, cleaning the garden, preparing meals for her employers and their young children, and, for some extra money (usually $10 or so), washing her employers' pleasure boat at their private dock at the end of the large backyard, where the couple's tennis court was located.

The fact that Ah Maa had no choice but to stay on Long Island 6 days a week gave her a desperate sense of isolation and loneliness. She would become very anxious when her employers sometimes came home late from work on Saturday evenings, thus delaying her trip to Flushing to meet her friends. "I'm trapped here, you see," Ah Maa often said to me during interviews, as if the enormous house were nothing but a large cage. The small Buddha shrine, the picture of *Gunyam* (the Goddess of Mercy),[4] and scores of family photos taped to the walls in her room never

---

[2]According to Takaki (1989), "the view of Asian immigrants as 'sojourners' and European immigrants as 'settlers' is both a mistaken notion and a widely held myth" (p. 10). Around the turn of the 20th century, an average of about 50% of certain European immigrants (such as those from the Great Britain, Italy, and Poland) returned to their homelands after coming to the United States.

[3]I did not ask the several dozen informants in this community whether they were documented immigrants, for I had no basis (nor any right) to assume or inquire about their legal status and therefore believed the act of asking the question was unjustifiable. However, Ah Maa and several of her friends did volunteer information during the course of my research that many of their friends were, like themselves, undocumented immigrants.

[4]Although Buddhism is an influential religion in the Chinese community in Malaysia, the Goddess of Mercy is considered the most popular deity among people in the community (Bunge, 1984).

seemed to give her enough company or consolation. The words "trapped," "bored," and "lonely" were always present in her consciousness during the many times over 2 years that I spoke with her at work. In fact, it was her enormously desperate sense of isolation and loneliness that drove her and people like her to karaoke.

Indeed, the sense of loneliness that engulfed Ah Maa was also shared by many of her friends. For example, although Anne was happy about getting her green card through the company she worked for, she has felt isolated ever since coming to the United States several years ago. Her green card did not stop her from contemplating returning to Malaysia in the future. "From the beginning, the U.S. isn't that good [for me]," Anne once told me with a short and dry chuckle. "Perhaps because I don't have any relatives here. I always feel lonely here, very lonely." A former cabaret singer in Malaysia and an administrative assistant at an accounting firm when I met her in Flushing in the early 1990s, Anne was not particularly thrilled about singing karaoke either. She preferred singing to live music. "Singing at karaoke parties," Anne said to me, "doesn't remind me of my life at the nightclubs." But karaoke was more than singing for her; it was a place where she came to know many compatriots, like those people I describe next.

## A Way to Forget It All

Ah Maa first came into contact with karaoke at a friend's birthday party at a club late in 1992. She had heard of karaoke before but she had never seen it or been to "the karaoke," as she liked to call the place where people sing karaoke. Ah Maa was very taken by the fact that in the club "all these people were so happy singing." She was a bit afraid of going up onto the stage area because it was all so new to her; it was so unlike singing (or humming) "those old songs I know" on her cassette player all by herself while doing her chores. She did not quite know what to do at first when her friends and new acquaintances suggested that she take the microphone. In much the same way as many people who are first exposed to karaoke, Ah Maa excused herself by saying, "I like to listen to you sing." On the inside, however, she acknowledged to me that she wished she could sing as well as everybody else at the club.

This particular karaoke birthday party introduced Ah Maa to a community that has brought much joy to her otherwise hard life. To begin with, Ah Maa could easily identify with many of the people she met at the club because they all came from Malaysia. Being Malaysian Chinese in New York City, where Chinese from China, Hong Kong, and Taiwan represent the majority of the general Chinese immigrant population, Ah Maa and her compatriots are essentially a minority within a minority. Such a double-minority status seems to have created a special

bond among them. Although people in this community never speak of
any intergroup tension with Chinese from other regional or ethnic
backgrounds, they mostly socialize with their compatriots. They share
similar social and even life histories. Indeed, one of the reported reasons
Ah Maa feels so comfortable with these people is because she does not
have to worry about explaining, among other things, her immigrant
status. They all know, and they all understand.

More specifically, however, it is the association with this community
of karaoke enthusiasts that gives Ah Maa the sense of self and social
identity that she longs for 6 days a week. Like many of her friends from
Malaysia, Ah Maa loves to sing, even though she really cannot sing well.
"I have a male goose's voice," she once suggested with a touch of
self-deprecating humor. But singing serves an important and explicit
function for Ah Maa:

> I've liked to sing all my life. I like to sing even when I work. Especially
> when I'm upset. I can forget my troubles. I concentrate on the lyrics and
> not other things. It's a relief. Try not to remember unhappy things. [She
> pauses to sing a verse from an old Cantonese pop song] *"Ji han yatseui
> gaak tinngaai"* ["Regretting that the ocean separates our worlds"]. Then
> I will forget my trouble. When I was back home, I sang after I had a fight
> with my *lougung*. I won't hide and cry. I sing even when I play mahjongg
> with friends.[5]

Singing karaoke has become a means for Ah Maa and many of her
compatriots to escape the humdrum routine of everyday life, a life that
is as alienating as it is confusing. "I don't know why I'm doing this—except I want to buy a house back home so I won't have to live in a
government housing project." Ah Maa's voice was full of doubt as much
as it was full of regret, if not guilt:

> After I came here [for the first time] . . . I cried for more than two years. I
> cried for more than two years but was afraid of telling my *lougung*. It's
> *chaileung* [sad]. My youngest daughter was very small, only 14 when I
> left. I felt I didn't fulfill my responsibility as a parent, as a *loumou*
> [mother]. [She's] so young! At the time [she] really needed [her] parents'
> guidance, no?

Perhaps the need for being with a family is also an important reason
why, as the oldest of all the people in this community, Ah Maa feels so
much at home with "those kids," "those little friends," as she calls them.
This warm feeling seems to be mutual among them. In fact, most of the
people in the community call her *kaima,* which means in Cantonese a

---

[5]This verse comes from one of the old songs Ah Maa has memorized, entitled *"Yatseui
Gaak Tinngaai"* ("The Ocean Separates Our Worlds").

woman whose position resembles that of an adopted mother—or god-mother in the West—even though it does not have any legal or religious connotation or ramification. They often treat Ah Maa when they get together for karaoke.

Unlike the private karaoke clubs in New Jersey or Cantonese opera musical associations in New York's Chinatown, people in this community do not organize themselves under any formal structure. Indeed, the concept of organization simply does not apply here. In the next section, I examine the informal karaoke scenes in which people in this interpretive community mostly congregate, and their social, economic, and ethnic implications.

## THE HANGOUT: AH TING AND HIS SMALL CLUB

On closer examination, one may better understand why people in this interpretive community do not have the kind of formal organization that people in the previous two interpretive communities enjoy (i.e., musical associations or *yamngok se* in the case of the community in New York's Chinatown and private karaoke clubs for the community in New Jersey). There are always a number of people in this current interpretive community who are transitory, either because it is time for them to return home or because they need to move on to another city for work. No one seems to stay in one place for very long. These people simply congregate at certain hangouts that are popular or customary among them, not always knowing whether all the same people will be there the next time.

With only a few exceptions, the majority of the people in this community do not have a karaoke machine at home. Because most of them are either single, or immigrated or traveled to the United States alone, they usually rent a room by themselves or share a small apartment with a few friends. Most of their living space at home is too small to accommodate many people for a karaoke gathering. Moreover, the noise from any karaoke gathering in such living arrangements might easily disturb neighbors. Finally, few people, even if they have the money, want to invest in a karaoke audiovisual system because it would mean an extra burden to carry on their trip from one stop to another.

### Ah Ting the Entrepreneur

The most popular hangouts for people in this community are the several Southeast Asian restaurants and few small karaoke clubs in Flushing. The restaurants and clubs that Ah Maa and her friends frequent are run by entrepreneurs who also come from a Malaysian Chinese background. Ah Ting, for instance, owned the club in Flushing's downtown where Ah

Maa was first introduced to karaoke and the community. Timmy, as another example, owned the restaurant where Ah Maa had her three karaoke birthday parties. Whereas these entrepreneurs do have the general public in mind, their compatriots are often the most consistent source of business. There is thus a symbiotic relationship between these entrepreneurs (or businesses) and the compatriots who patronize them. The community manifests itself when the people congregate and socialize at these hangouts, and these businesses exist because the people patronize them.

Ah Ting is typical of younger immigrants from Malaysia who never seem to give up on any new entrepreneurial venture, even if the last one did not work out. Early in the 1990s, with whatever he had left or accumulated from other previous businesses and loans from friends, Ah Ting opened a karaoke club on Roosevelt Avenue, one of the busiest business centers in all of Flushing. On the street level, there are always rapid streams of people going in and out of the numerous groceries, ethnic Asian restaurants, supermarkets, bakeries, and newsstands.

At the time of the club's opening, karaoke was becoming a popular form of entertainment among many in the Chinese American immigrant communities in the New York metropolitan area. When Ah Ting's club opened its doors for business, it became a magnet for many in Flushing's ethnic Malaysian Chinese community. Because of the club, Ah Ting became, almost immediately, the center of attention among the people who later befriended Ah Maa. It is difficult to estimate how many Malaysians are living in the Flushing area because no New York City statistics exist that pertain specifically to this group. Of course, undocumented or transient immigrants do not make such an estimate any easier either. However, this never seemed to concern Ah Ting, who was in his late 20s at the time, when he wondered whether he would attract enough customers to his club. In fact, were it not for his network of compatriots and acquaintances in the area, he might not have felt confident enough to invest in the club to begin with.

## The Club on Roosevelt Avenue

Ah Ting's club was on the top floor of a three-story walk-up overlooking Roosevelt Avenue. It was always locked behind a security gate. The club was, by all measures, a very small one, with a maximum capacity of approximately 40 to 45 patrons at any given time. Compared to other fancier clubs in town, the physical arrangement in Ah Ting's club can be considered as elementary. In the middle of the rectangular floor space, which resembled a small studio apartment, were two rows of about five tables each, running along the two long walls. The back of the club, facing the street, was the stage area that had a front-projection monitor screen, two microphones on stands, and a small television monitor (for the performers to follow the lyrics) with its back to the audience area. There was a disco-style reflective ball hanging over the dance floor in the center of the room.

A few steps from the entrance was the front of the club, where patrons paid their admission fee. Next to the reception area was the control booth, where the karaoke disc jockey showcased the selection of songs and played them according to customers' requests.

Like other such clubs in the area, Ah Ting's club operated on two shifts. There were the tea dance hours in the afternoon for those who could or would spend a couple of hours during the day relaxing. However, most of Ah Ting's business occurred during the evening hours; the busiest evenings of the week were always Friday and Saturday.

The way in which customers' performances were managed at such a club was a matter of standard operation. When the customers at a table ordered their first round of drinks, the waiter deposited small pieces of paper and a songbook on the table. Patrons at the table could then write down the number of a song on a piece of paper, which would be picked up by the waiter. After the karaoke disc jockey received the selection(s), she would either play the songs in the order they were received or, if there were many people in the club, played one song at a time per table on a rotating basis.

Because most of the customers attracted to Ah Ting's club come from a similar social and ethnic background, there is something of a communal feeling among the patrons. Friendly or even sympathetic interactions between people at different tables are not uncommon, especially among those who patronize the club on weekend nights. In the next section, I analyze how these interactions can be viewed as ethnically based communal experiences that echo the social and personal worlds of the people in this interpretive community. The analysis concentrates on the experience of Ah Maa and her close friends in the context of Ah Ting's club.

### SEE YOU ONLY IN DREAMS: A COMMUNAL CRY?

Because Ah Maa cannot read, her repertoire of karaoke songs is limited to those she has memorized. Before she came into contact with karaoke, Ah Maa knew quite a few old songs from her many years of humming them, even though she had memorized just about half the lyrics to each of those songs. Most of the songs she recalled for me depict desperation, loneliness, or other sadness, such as "I'm the Only One Who Is Lonely," "Not Returning Home Today," and "Don't Abandon Me." But Ah Maa can only sing a few songs with karaoke because many of the old songs she has memorized are not available in karaoke form, or she has never chanced upon them if they are available. Among the few available karaoke pieces are a Mandarin song, *"Meichiu Chia K'afei"* ("Fine Wine Mixed With Coffee") and a Cantonese song, *"Yatseui Gaak Tinngaai"* ("The Ocean Separates Our Worlds"). These are two all-time favorites in the Chinese-speaking world that depict, respectively, falling out of love, and separation. Ah Maa began to hum these two songs when she first encountered them at Ah Ting's club.

Very soon after she heard (and saw) those two songs performed in karaoke, Ah Maa called her husband in Malaysia, asking him to record the songs on an audiocassette tape for her. Dutifully, he did. Repeatedly, Ah Maa listened to her husband's tape that week until she had memorized the lyrics. She then went to Ah Ting's club for her debut performance.

Ah Maa and Ah Ting struck up a close friendship soon after she was brought over to the club for her friend's birthday party. It is still unclear to Ah Maa why Ah Ting "has been so nice to me," but after the first two visits, Ah Ting stopped charging her an admission fee and often brought her drinks. Like many of Ah Maa's friends, Ah Ting became her helper at the club, for in the beginning of Ah Maa's debut period she always asked someone to sing with her:

> Every time I went up, I would take either Ah Ting or someone else with me. When I wasn't sure or didn't understand [the words], I lowered my voice. If I knew, I sang loudly. You know my voice is very loud. If I know [the words], I sing loud. I sing loudly for others [to enjoy]. If I don't know [the words], I won't sing loud for people to hear [laugh], afraid of them hearing it.

Ah Maa once drafted me to help her sing *"Yatseui Gaak Tinngaai"* when Ah Ting was busy with something else. Ah Maa held my left hand the whole time the song was in progress. I could feel her excitement and intensity growing when she could follow the lyrics, for during those verses, she squeezed my hand. She stayed just about half a second behind me when she was not feeling confident. I sensed at the time that she was trying very hard to recognize the shape of the Chinese lyrics running across the bottom of the screen while listening intently to the words coming from my mouth. I could feel the energy radiating from her.

Ah Maa sang those same few songs every time she went to Ah Ting's club. For a period of time, almost without exception, she would team with Ah Ting for "The Ocean Separates Our Worlds." "You know," Ah Maa explained, "Ah Ting's wife was in Malay[sia] to give birth to their baby. My *lougung* was also in Malay. Ah Ting was here, I was here." Ah Maa liked to sing the song with Ah Ting partially because she believed the song struck as responsive a chord in him as it did in her.

## The Unaccompanied Love Song

But what seemed to bind together many more of their friends and even some patrons at other tables is another song that Ah Maa always sang at Ah Ting's club. It is an unaccompanied Cantonese song that Ah Maa's husband wrote for her a couple of years after she left Malaysia that he called "See You in My Dream." By Ah Maa's account, her husband wrote the song as a way of reminding her of his love for her and encouraging her to return home soon. Because she cannot read, Ah Maa's husband recorded the song on a cassette tape. Ah Maa listened to and hummed the song on the tape over and over again long before she came into contact with karaoke; that is, before she had karaoke as a context to share the song with anyone other than herself and her husband. Her raspy voice added a strong dose of sadness to the lyrics:

> Through teary eyes I see you in my dreams.
> Our separation already slipped by the Spring and Autumn.
> Will we reunite soon?
> My beloved wife, please maintain your love for me.
> I ask the heaven but it doesn't say a word,
> I ask the earth but it remains silent.
> We are separated like two lost swallows, and
> don't know when we will reunite.
> Remember how deeply in love we were.
> Now we are separated, tears running down my face.
> What will happen in our next life
> can't be known in our current life.
> Time flies and will never return.
> Let me say to you, my beloved wife
> don't be worried or sad.
> Wish we have heaven's blessing
> that our love in this life won't end.

At one point, in her conversation with me, Ah Maa explained her husband's intention behind the song in something like a monologue. She played the roles of herself, her husband, and a third-person narrator deciphering the meaning of the conversation:

> He asked me [over the phone], "*Loupo* [wife], do you know what my song means? Do you feel anything?" Feeling means whether you have tears in your eyes. "I sang the song for you, what feeling do you have?" [he asked]. That means if you know the meaning of the song you will have feeling or will cry. Right? It's really sad that you have to see each other only in dreams. I said [to him], "I know." He then asked me, "Did you cry?" "Yes, I did." [He commented,] "Well, then you still remember your *lougung*. If you don't remember the song, you won't remember your *lougung*. That's not bad. You still remember me. You remember the song." [He] asked me

if I shed my tears. I said to him, "I did. Your song is very sad. Why did you
write the song for me? Who taught you to write it? Did you read it in the
newspaper?" He said, "No, I just have too much time on my hands." He
then asked me, "Would you come back because of the song?" "No," I said.
"No matter how you use your song to move me, it's difficult. I'm determined
to stay in the States. I will stay for a full five years before I will go back.
I'm used to life here."

Although Ah Maa did not tell her husband the truth (about her being
used to life in the United States), the song was apparently therapeutic.
It became her medium to reach out for sympathy and acknowledgment
of her misery, from the community of people who shared a similar fate
to hers.

> I sang the song every time I went [to karaoke]. They shed tears for me.
> Many people, whether they know me or not, said this is a very sad song
> that your [my] husband wrote. When I went up I would tell people. I said,
> "So many of you little friends." I'm the oldest there, the oldest. I said, "So
> many of you little friends, do you want to listen to a song that has no music?
> My *lougung* sent me the song from Malay. If you're interested, I can sing
> it for you." Of course, every one was clapping hands; they didn't know what
> song it would be. Want to hear it, right? Every time I sang the song, these
> people would imitate, "Ahhh . . . *loupo* ["my wife"] . . . oh!" Ah Tin did that
> too [laugh]. Every time I sang the song, Ah Ting would provide background
> music by making noises [imitating some Cantonese opera instruments].
> Making faces. Sometimes people asked me to sing. Some people didn't
> understand it. They know Chinese [Cantonese] but they don't understand
> [the connotation of] what I'm singing about. People who understood would
> have tears in their eyes when they heard me sing the song. They said, "It's
> sad. You're separated from your husband only to see each other in your
> dream." Isn't it sad?

Were it not for karaoke, and Ah Ting's club in particular, which laid out
for her a dramaturgical (if not dramatic) structure for such expression,
Ah Maa might not have been able to find a voice that she could project
and that would resonate among her compatriots. Besides, it would have
seemed out of place if Ah Maa were to vocalize herself over mahjongg
games. At one level, Ah Ting's club gave her compatriots a conducive
communal environment to savor the bitter experience of separation that
was as realistic to them as it was to Ah Maa. "You feel happy when people
respond to you and share the feeling you express," Anne, the former
cabaret singer, once told me.

This section has analyzed how vocal participation plays a part in the
expression and sharing of certain communal sentiments among some
members of this interpretive community. In the next section, I analyze

how some other people in this interpretive community maintain their membership through what can be called silent participation.

## JUST TO BE WITH SOMEONE: THE SILENT PARTICIPANTS IN KARAOKE SCENES

Although there are no shortage of karaoke enthusiasts in this interpretive community, not all of the people are avid singers. In fact, many people in the community who go to the weekend karaoke parties are silent participants, who support but do not engage actively in the vocalized production of performances. The reason they go to these events seems to be their desire to be a part of their compatriots' activities.

Ah Ting's club experienced at least one armed robbery during the few years it was in business. Ah Maa was there when the armed robbery occurred ("I was under the table the whole time"). The incident did not deter her or any of her friends from going back to the club every Saturday night. Nevertheless, Ah Ting closed the club late in 1993 due to fire code violations that he could not correct. A few months after the club closed, he opened a hair salon elsewhere in Flushing. The basement of the salon featured a waiting room with a karaoke set-up which Ah Maa and her friends visited fairly regularly. A back room in the basement offered some space for people to play mahjongg or cards, from which Ah Ting drew a commission. But three armed robberies, apparently attracted by the money circulating in this room, forced Ah Ting to close his salon.

### The Karaoke Rooms in Timmy's Restaurant

In the intervening months after Ah Ting's club was closed and before his salon was opened, Ah Maa and the other people in the community began to shift their attention to a few Southeast Asian restaurants in the area where they could sing karaoke. Timmy's restaurant just off Main Street was one of the favorite hangouts for Ah Maa and her friends, partly because of Timmy's hospitality and partly because of the two karaoke rooms in the restaurant's basement. In his early 40s, the bespectacled Timmy always wore a slight smile on his face and never seemed to raise his voice to anyone. He wore the black pants, white shirt, and black tie common among Chinese American restaurant managers.

Like many Chinese restaurants in New York, Timmy's jumped on the karaoke bandwagon early in the 1990s in an attempt to keep up with the competition for a seemingly shrinking clientele in the midst of a recession, when scores of restaurants in Chinatown and Flushing were going into or out of business. Timmy's restaurant, like many such restaurants in the area, imposed no extra charge for using the karaoke rooms; he was just happy that his karaoke rooms could bring in extra business during dinner hours.

To Timmy's compatriots, the karaoke rooms in the basement provided an inexpensive, convenient, and therefore welcome environment for meeting their friends. Of course, playing mahjongg serves similar social functions for many in the community, but players also stand to lose their hard-earned money. Getting together over dinner is also a long-standing social institution among Chinese. Although a dinner at the restaurant provides a context for social interaction, the evening invariably ends when the dinner is over. This may be one important reason why karaoke has become such a popular after-dinner social entertainment among Chinese. Karaoke helps Chinese people to extend their social life and interaction beyond or after the dining table. After all, karaoke affords people an effective means to avoid having to talk about their day-to-day existence, especially if this is something they would rather not talk about.

Contrary to the perception that people who go to karaoke love to sing, there are many others who enjoy themselves at karaoke gatherings even though they cannot sing, do not sing, or do not like to sing karaoke. The experience of some of the guests at Ah Maa's second karaoke birthday party in the summer of 1993 (which made its first appearance in the first section of this chapter) offers an interesting case study of how some people in this community maintain their bond with others in karaoke scenes through silent participation.

## Silent Participation as Social Bonding

As more and more guests went down to the restaurant's basement, the air in the karaoke party room was becoming thicker and more suffocating with cigarette smoke. A couple of the waiters who earlier in the evening were sitting idly upstairs began to serve scores of dishes: sweetly marinated chicken bits wrapped in banana leaves, beef stew in steamy curry sauce, cold thin rice noodles (with crushed peanuts, onion, pepper, and shrimp in lemon juice), hot and spicy shrimp, and so forth. A bucket of beer cans buried in ice cubes was also brought in. Some of the guests picked up their plastic plates and forks for the food on the table, and others were still chatting amongst themselves. Ah Maa was busy giving a red paper money bag that contained a dollar bill and a raffle number to each guest. She would later give out a few extra gifts to those whose numbers were drawn. Ah Maa thought this would bring people good luck.

Several of the karaoke enthusiasts intermittently took to the stage area to belt out their favorites and Ah Ting occasionally acted as if he were the event's master of ceremonies. Ah Jun, a cashier at a grocery store, and her boyfriend Ah Sing, a machinist in his mid-20s, were among the more active performers during the evening. They always stayed very close to one another in this small space, holding each other's hands tightly. The several times in the evening when they actually were separated were when Ah Sing had to get up to the machine to pick their love songs. Similarly, Hung Sai and his girlfriend Jeanne were another popular pair, especially when Hung Sai took to the microphone. A carpenter by trade, Hung Sai is an accomplished amateur singer and has participated in several karaoke singing contests.

Ah Mei, meanwhile, was all by herself even in the presence of her husband, Ah Yung, with whom she worked at a garment factory. In their mid-20s, they already had two children who were left behind in Malaysia. Ah Mei was the more outgoing of the two. Whereas Ah Yung dressed blandly, Ah Mei seemed to favor more flashy clothes, such as the red miniskirt she wore for this party. She loved to sing either at home after work with their own karaoke machine, or at parties with friends. Ah Mei sang her songs so strenuously that she literally was losing her voice by the middle of the evening. Her husband, on the other hand, seemed to prefer sitting there sipping his soda. When asked if he liked to sing karaoke—a standard ice-breaker at karaoke parties—the only, very quiet answer Ah Yung gave was: "Ah Mei likes to sing." Ah Yung is what can be considered a silent participant.

Ah Yung was not the only silent participant at the party, however. If someone at the time mistakenly unplugged the stereo system, thereby cutting off the loud music and singing that filled the room, one might come to the sudden realization that a lot of the guests at the party were actually not making any sounds at all. There were always 10 or so people at the party who seemed to have no desire to engage in any conversation or performance at all. They did greet Ah Maa and the other guests. They did say a few words to, or exchange pleasantries with, one another now and then, although they seemed to do so just to punctuate their long silence. A few of them even hummed, albeit very quietly, to some of the music while sipping on their drinks or when no one was in close proximity to them. However, most of their activity at the party was comprised of their mere presence.

Indeed, of the 60 or so guests attending Ah Maa's second party, about 45 of them never participated in the singing at all although they likely knew beforehand that it was a karaoke party. I attempted to solicit from these people their reason for not participating in the singing. Several of them suggested to me that they did not know all the people at the party and did not feel comfortable enough to sing before strangers. Some people excused themselves by saying that they could not sing. But most of them simply said that it was fine with them just sitting there listening to other people sing. Cathy, Ah Maa's painfully shy, widowed *kaineui* ("adopted" daughter), is an interesting example. She paid for Ah Maa's first karaoke birthday party although she could not attend. But at Ah Maa's second and third parties, as well as several other karaoke scenes thereafter, I observed that Cathy mostly sat quietly with her friends. This led me to believe that many of the silent participants at the party, like Cathy, were there just to show their friendship to Ah Maa by attending her birthday party and simply did not have any intention of singing.

At one level, it appeared to me that the presence of the silent participants at the party served what Bronislaw Malinowski (1956) considered the phatic function of communication; that is, the maintenance of relationship between participants in an interaction—rather than the transfer of information between them. Good friends who spend hours chatting on the telephone do not necessarily pay much attention to the specific information or hard facts being exchanged. An important aspect of human communication is the maintenance of human relationships through continued interaction. The act of chatting or having a conversation is, in and of itself, an important everyday ritual of maintaining contact and relationships with others. Indeed, many of the silent participants at Ah Maa's birthday party were there not to sing, for they did not sing, or to exchange information, for they did not talk much either. They were apparently there to signal and maintain their friendship and membership in the community. But unlike friends chatting on the phone, many people in Ah Maa's karaoke birthday party maintained the bonding among themselves by being silent members in the audience. Thus, they contributed an important element in the maintenance of karaoke scenes, at the same time that they maintained their friendship and connection to others.

Of course, there are people in this interpretive community who want more than just mutual copresence. For these people, indeed, karaoke is an excuse to hide from the reality that they otherwise face as a matter of routine. Karaoke provides these people with the situation to construct and experience fantasies not found in their everyday lives. The next and final section of this chapter analyzes how a few of Ah Maa's friends at her third birthday party used karaoke to construct and live in a temporary, dramaturgical event. As analyzed in more detail, the following karaoke scene entails the imaginative use of mass-produced popular culture products in the construction and maintenance of human relationships. It also symbolizes the participants' attempt to attain some melodramatic digression into a reality that is not part of their—or anyone's—everyday lives. The analysis begins with my encounter with a couple of the episode's key participants whose living conditions reveal part of their specific social and economic background.

## A LATE-NIGHT KARAOKE EXCURSION: TRAVELING BETWEEN REALITY AND MELODRAMA

Before I went to Ah Maa's third karaoke birthday party, she asked me to help pick up a couple of her young friends, Kitty and Susan, from their home. Ah Maa routinely stayed with Kitty and Susan after their Saturday night parties, before returning to Long Island late on Sunday. At the time of my visit, Kitty and Susan had just gotten back from their first trip home to Malaysia. They were renting a very small and sparsely furnished room on the second floor of a two-family wood-frame house on a narrow residential street only a short walking distance from downtown Flushing. The landlord did not live in the house. It was difficult to determine how many tenants lived there, but it seemed that all the rooms were occupied by people who did not even know each other's first name.

### Susan and Kitty: The Travelers

I encountered Susan in front of the house as she was coming home from the subway station after her day's work as a waitress in midtown Manhattan. Having seen me at several other gatherings, Susan acknowledged me but her steps were slow and somewhat heavy as she was climbing the stairs after a long day at work. Although Kitty and Susan are not related, Susan addressed Kitty as *jeje* (elder sister), an intimate form of address, connoting a relatively high level of friendship. Like Susan, Kitty grew up in a big working-class family, with several brothers and sisters in Malaysia. A few of Kitty's siblings were already married and had moved away from home. Those who were left behind worked to help sustain the livelihood of the family. Although both Kitty and Susan are very young, in their mid- to late-20s, I can feel the enormous pride and dignity they have for themselves, as they always seem to swallow any complaints that may give away the hard life they have to endure.

Kitty and Susan studied for a few years in a public high school. Although they did not study Chinese extensively, Kitty and Susan learned to speak a few Chinese dialects while at home. This was helped by their consumption of imported popular entertainment, such as Hong Kong and Taiwanese movies, television programs, and videos. They also were avid readers of popular novels from Hong Kong and Taiwan, particularly romance novels, that helped them to keep up with their reading in Chinese.

It is interesting to note that one of the popular writers, Connie, whose romance novels Kitty and Susan read, is an active member in a private karaoke club in New Jersey. Although Connie's novels bring them together in a writer–reader relationship, Kitty and Susan belong to a drastically different social class from Connie. Recently, Connie informed the audience at a large karaoke gala that she publishes one novel a month. She apparently lives a stable and extremely affluent life, with a husband who is successful in business and a child studying at an elite college. It is a plentiful and fanciful life, unlike that of Kitty and Susan and many of their contemporaries, who are quite unsure of their futures.

The following scene illustrates how Susan, with collaboration from her counterparts, constructed a karaoke episode in which a melodramatic digression from everyday reality was pursued. The scene entails the spontaneous and imaginative use of mass-produced popular culture products to construct and maintain a fantasy relationship—one that bears a certain resemblance to the kind of melodramatic relationships in Connie's romance novels—in the middle of a real-life social gathering.

### A Melodrama in Karaoke Terms

Timmy, the restaurant owner, invited only a handful of guests to Ah Maa's third karaoke birthday dinner party. It was held in the same karaoke room as before, except this time most of the chairs were folded and there was only a round table standing several feet away from the karaoke machine. Among the guests at the table were two contractors, Denny and Ah Dong, both in their late 30s. Denny, a Hong Kong Cantonese, owns a construction company. His girlfriend was out of town that weekend and he was there at the party to *wet* (pronounced with the "t" swallowed), a slang term in Cantonese used among many in this community to mean, roughly, have fun. Denny had met Susan at a previous karaoke party and the two seemed to have developed a fondness for each other. They arranged to sit next to each other. Sitting to the left of Denny was Ah Ting, whose seat was the closest to the karaoke system; he would frequently leave his seat to select songs for the rest of the guests. During most of the evening, the guests sang from their seats. Next to Ah Ting were Kitty and Ah Dong. In addition to Ah Maa, the guest of honor, a few regulars in the community were also there, such as Cathy, Ah Maa's very shy "adopted" daughter, and Ah Jun and Ah Sing, the couple who were madly in love with each other and who would sing nothing but love ballads.

Ah Dong was the only new face at the table, so Timmy was obliged to introduce him to everyone. When he introduced Ah Dong to Susan by asking, "Have you two met?" Ah Dong suggested that Susan looked familiar to him. But this slight suggestion, which could have been a very subtle pick-up line, was all that it took for an interesting and quite dramatic episode to play itself out. The guests were expecting a simple answer from Susan, such as "no" or "where?", but she came up with a surprising response. In a playful tone of voice, she said to Ah Dong, "Oh, yeah, we must have been lovers before, but how come we can't even recognize each other now?" Susan's response drew a wave of laughter from the rest of the guests. After a pause and a glance at Susan, and seemingly not wanting to be outdone, Ah Dong picked up on Susan's line, saying "How bad have I been! That must have been in our previous lives." These words could well have come from the kind of romance novels that Susan and Kitty enjoy reading in their spare time. "Oh yes, in our previous lives," Susan went along about their fictitious romance in a flirtatious voice.

After that exchange, the interaction between Ah Dong and Susan continued across the table as they clowned around about their "past relationship" as if to relive the romance again. Although Denny was the center of Susan's attention at the beginning of the party, he seemed to be a bit out of favor after Ah Dong came onto the scene. Denny did make a few attempts to become part of the conversation between Susan and Ah Dong, but he did not make much of an inroad. The more he tried, the more he seemed to take the role of a supporting cast member in the episode. After a few drinks, Susan and Ah Dong began to sing a few Cantonese and Mandarin pop songs together.

Although there may be several reasons why Denny did not do well in this episode, part of the explanation can be found in karaoke terms. Essentially, Denny did not share the same karaoke repertoire that Susan and Ah Dong had in common. Similar to many high school students in Hong Kong back in the early 1970s, he was more interested in U. S. pop songs than he was in local musical fare. As a result, he seemed to have a rather limited knowledge of Cantonese and Mandarin songs. Unfortunately for him, Cantonese and Mandarin songs were exactly the mainstay of the karaoke music collection in that restaurant. Therefore, Denny's involvement in the make-believe affair, his competition for Susan's attention via karaoke, or both, could only be marginal.

Susan and Ah Dong were familiar with the same repertoire of Mandarin and Cantonese pop songs—those from both the oldies category and the more contemporary fare. So whenever Ah Dong had a chance to pick a song after other guests, he signaled to Susan to join in by passing her the second microphone. At one point, Ah Dong took Denny's temporarily vacated seat and was sitting very close to Susan. A few moments later, the line between reality and fantasy blurred as they sang a Mandarin song, "Lover." One of the lines goes, "Lover, lover, how can I forget you!"

As the lyrics ran across the bottom of the monitor screen, an actor and an actress posed as lovers in the rest of the video frame. Meanwhile, Ah Dong and Susan sang the song holding their hands tightly and pressing their heads close to each other. They sang in this manner over the next several duets. At times, it was difficult to discern whether the two were simply acting out the scene on the screen, falling for each other at the party, or truly rekindling a previous relationship.

However, about an hour and a half later, Susan gradually disengaged herself from Ah Dong as she joined the rest of the guests in group singing of a couple of songs. Ah Dong seemed to show a degree of surprise and unease at the breakup but nonetheless maintained a low profile and did not pursue further, at least not to my eyes. At about 4:30 in the morning, Susan, Kitty, and Ah Maa bade farewell to their compatriots, left the scene together, and returned to the small room in the wood-frame house where the two mattresses on the floor were awaiting them.

I later asked Ah Maa about Susan's relationship with Ah Dong. She told me that they had never met before that party. Susan simply liked to play (or flirt). The make-believe romance never lived beyond the dramaturgical confine of that karaoke scene.

This episode at Ah Maa's third birthday party in 1993 is another interesting example of how participants can use both karaoke's dramaturgical frame and the repertoire of karaoke music to create an imaginary scenario. Susan and Ah Dong acted out a communicative event that was at once melodramatic and unconventional. Karaoke-based social interactions are unconventional because they contain the components of music and video. More importantly, they incorporate the direct involvement of people on an in-the-moment basis in performing or becoming part of some inherently dramatic material. To a certain extent, this kind of dramatic potential makes human interaction in a karaoke scene unpredictable.

The dialogues between Ah Dong and Susan, in the manner in which they were uttered and performed, bore conspicuous resemblance to dialogues used in certain Chinese popular romance novels or Cantonese operas. In fact, Ah Dong and Susan used popular culture products—that is, karaoke music and videos—to write their script on the spot. They improvised and performed their roles and acts as the scene progressed in real-time.

Of course, by characterizing such karaoke-based episodes in the manner I have, I am not suggesting that the interactions are by nature idiosyncratic. Certain rules of decorum traditionally followed at birthday parties and social dinners—such as toasting the host (as a token of appreciation for his or her hospitality) or other guests at the table (as a matter of common courtesy) when a new dish is served, or positioning the guest of honor at the center of attention—still applied in the previous episode. Nevertheless, there is a loose dramaturgical context for karaoke-based interactions. Imbedded in every karaoke-based social interaction are dramatic and unpredictable turns; each actual scene results from imaginative uses of karaoke for the construction, maintenance, and transformation of participants' social identities.

## A SUMMARY ANALYSIS

People in this third interpretive community, such as Ah Maa, Susan, and the silent participants, construct karaoke scenes as a temporary social and symbolic heaven where they can escape from a sense of entrapment, the everyday repetition and humdrum routine, and the reality of being in isolation. As a minority within a minority, these people's social space is both limited and marginalized. The illegal immigrant status of many of these people has narrowed their economic possibilities, which further inhibits their social reach. Singing karaoke is more than just entertainment to them. They use karaoke to create certain social spaces to keep in touch with people who share similar life histories, through either vocal or silent participation. These are spaces where people in the community, even in the most adverse of social and economic conditions, can have a voice of their own, a voice of self-assurance and of connection. The use of karaoke here speaks to people's need to have an escape, or therapeutic mechanism, that gives them access to a way of life otherwise absent from their everyday existence, even if the escape can only be temporary.

# 6

# Karaoke and the Construction of Identity

This book has been concerned with understanding the interaction between the media audience and karaoke. Its analysis has focused on the various ways that people with different ethnic, social, economic, and personal frames of reference engage karaoke as a cultural practice. The analysis is based on ethnographic case studies of three interpretive communities of first-generation Chinese American immigrants, with data focusing on how they adopt karaoke in the construction, maintenance, and transformation of social identity.

As part of the theoretical framework, I delineated in chapter 1 that, as a technology for communication, karaoke is the material embodiment of the cultural practice of amateur social singing. As White (1962) suggested in his study of technology and social change, the introduction of a new technology into a society merely opens a door. How a technology is used and what consequences may result from its use depend as much on the general social conditions of adoption as on the individual needs and aspirations of the people who adopt it. The door that karaoke opens involves possibilities for the construction and maintenance of social membership through amateur participatory singing. People who choose to enter the door have to explore and determine for themselves what they want to do with these possibilities. How these possibilities are eventually realized is the result of, to quote Carey (1995) once again, "the complex interplay between a technology and the entire political, economic, and cultural infrastructure built up in relation to the articulation of a way of life" (p. 84).

The divergent voices and experiences of the three interpretive communities of first-generation Chinese American immigrants analyzed in this book speak directly to this complex interplay among various social, economic, political, ethnic, and technological forces in the articulation of cultures or ways of life in the diaspora. In this concluding chapter, I first briefly summarize how karaoke is engaged as part of the social experience of the three interpretive communities. I then consider these karaoke experiences as various expressions of people's ethnicity, social and economic class, and gendered relations. Thereafter, I discuss some of the theoretical implications of these findings for our understanding of the relationship between karaoke (and other similar technologies for communication) and society.

## THREE VOICES: THREE ARTICULATIONS OF
## LIFE IN THE DIASPORA

Three different ways to engage karaoke as cultural practices have emerged from the analysis of the case studies in the preceding three chapters. The first interpretive community consists of Hong Kong Cantonese immigrants active in New York's Chinatown who use karaoke as a cultural connection. But while karaoke provides them with a link to an older cultural practice, the singing of Cantonese opera songs (*yutkuk*), it also helps to transform how *yutkuk* is sung and presented in the contemporary social and technological environment. Personal musical competence is also influenced when the performer makes a shift from singing *yutkuk* with live music to singing with prepackaged karaoke music. Nevertheless, people in this community use karaoke to expand their social life worlds beyond the walls of their *yamngok se* and to create a ritual performance context for their compatriots in the Chinatown neighborhoods. In the process, they also help keep part of their musical tradition and ritual alive in the diaspora.

The second interpretive community is composed of Taiwanese immigrants active in affluent suburbs of New Jersey who engage karaoke as an expression of their wealth and social class. How they organize their private karaoke clubs and galas and their approach to their karaoke experiences reveals a conspicuous degree of corporate managerial mannerisms and a competitive drive. These might have been acquired as part of the members' professional ascents, and run parallel to the way they have been assimilated into the U.S. economic mainstream. Members of this community manage their leisure activity in a way that resembles their work in the corporate environment. The structure of their karaoke spaces also manifests a patriarchal social and moral worldview.

The third interpretive community is represented by certain Malaysian Chinese active in the Flushing area of Queens in New York City who employ karaoke as an escape mechanism. Multiply marginalized by their relatively low economic status and (for some) undocumented immigrant status, and as a minority within a minority, people in this interpretive community find solace in the communal webs of karaoke. Through karaoke, they construct a voice of their own that articulates their human condition, their alienation, their loneliness, and the absence of recognition from the larger social environment. Through imaginative uses, karaoke is transformed into a sort of therapeutic heaven where they can find relief from their isolated, humdrum routine.

On closer analysis, there are certain underlying factors that help construct and distinguish these experiences and voices. In reference to the initial theoretical, historical, and sociological discussion in chapters 1 and 2, the following three sections synthesize how the three karaoke experiences are expressions of the diverse ethnicities and economic experiences, as well as contrasting gendered social practices of the community members.

### Expressions of Ethnicity

The diverse karaoke experiences analyzed in this book express the complex ethnic composition of people across the three interpretive communities. According to W. W. Isajiw (1974), a people's ethnicity "is a matter of a double boundary, a boundary from within, maintained by the socialization process, and a boundary from without established by the process of intergroup relations" (p. 122). As minority people in multiethnic America, these first-generation Chinese immigrants have to constantly negotiate with people in the dominant society and other minorities to establish and maintain their social space and representation. They maintain a strong tie with people from similar backgrounds, especially when facing overt and covert racism or racial ignorance and hostility in the larger society. Meanwhile, regionalism plays an important role in how many Chinese immigrants define or establish their intragroup membership and bonding. Historically, as I have documented, many Chinese immigrants made their adjustment by staying close together for social acceptance, economic survival, political protection, and cultural familiarity.

This is not to say that people in the three interpretive communities necessarily go through the same assimilation process. Whereas many Chinese Americans remain in their social and ethnic enclaves (like many people in Mrs. Chung and Ah Maa's communities), many others acquire and maintain a pluralistic profile (like many people in John's community). On closer scrutiny, however, even the extent of assimilation achieved by John and his compatriots is not complete or thorough. Assimilation, according to R. T. Schaefer (1979), is the process whereby an immigrant or immigrant group acquires the traits of the dominant society and is ultimately absorbed into that society. There is no doubt that people in John's community have acquired some traits of the dominant economic structure, such as corporate managerial mannerisms, professionalism, a material lifestyle, and so forth. But they largely remain with people from their ethnic and regional background for the maintenance of their personal life world. Recall what Louis, the president of a private karaoke club, said: "Frankly, there are interactions with Americans at the professional or business level. But when it comes to personal life, it is seldom that Chinese enter the social network of Americans, or vice-versa."

One should not overgeneralize Louis' experience to represent the experience of all first-generation Chinese immigrants, but my observation of their karaoke practice and attendance to their testimonies leads me to conclude that Louis' attitude is shared by many people in the three communities. They are not ethnocentric, nor are they xenophobic—for they do interact to varying degrees with people from outside of their own ethnic background at various points. As first-generation immigrants, they simply do not share the same social and life history with people who otherwise grew up in the dominant society and the different ways of life it embodies. Therefore, it is understandable that certain first-generation immigrants cannot, do not, or will not fully identify with people in the dominant society at the social (personal life) level. Accordingly, there is reason to wonder if assimilation—in Schaefer's (1979) terms—can ever be accomplished.

People's regional backgrounds also play a role in their musical choice, which creates boundaries of its own. For example, people in Mrs. Chung's community use mostly Cantonese opera and popular songs from Hong Kong. Coming from a regional and linguistic background in Taiwan, people in John's community use mostly Mandarin and Taiwanese songs. The presence of Japanese-language or Japanese-tinged music (such as *enka*-style Taiwanese songs) also reveals a degree of Japanese cultural influence in the lives of some of these people. It is a trait largely absent from the other two communities. Finally, the karaoke music used by people in Ah Maa's community tends to be a mix of Cantonese, Mandarin, and Taiwanese songs. Cantonese, Mandarin, and Taiwanese are part of these people's language community in Malaysia; media products from Hong Kong and Taiwan encode these three Chinese dialects.

At the level of East–West cross-cultural consumption of karaoke music, John's community seems the most pluralistic of the three. On the average, about one sixth to one fifth of the songs performed at the large-scale karaoke galas are English-language (notably American) songs. To the contrary, I rarely hear members of the other two communities sing English-language songs. Of course, this fact alone does not suggest that people in these two communities cannot sing such songs. It may be just a matter of their own musical preference, partly defined by their personal and regional experience although the nonselection of English songs is widespread in these two communities.

In short, the karaoke practices of the three interpretive communities, including their specific choices of music, are expressions of the distinct ethnic and regional backgrounds of the people as they construct and maintain social membership. The fact that people in these three communities socialize mostly with others of a similar regional background is indicative of the important role that regionalism plays in the construction and maintenance of Chinese identity, that Chinese are not just Chinese, but Chinese from "where." Of course, it is important to note that the experiences of these first-generation immigrants cannot and should not be generalized to represent how their offspring in the diaspora might construct, maintain, or negotiate their ethnic identity—for the latter are acculturated in a different society, a different region.[1] Moreover, they might also have views of their parents' homeland or cultures that are different from what their parents have in mind or practice.

## Expressions of Class

The karaoke practices of the three interpretive communities are also expressions of the people's divergent economic experiences, at both the inter- as well as intracommunity levels. At the intercommunity level, the three interpretive communities represent three economic experiences or classes in Chinese America. People in John's community belong to an upper middle to upper class; they are economically accomplished and fairly well-assimilated into the U. S. mainstream. Members in Mrs. Chung's community, in contrast, belong to a middle to lower middle class, living comfortably but remaining mostly in the economic enclave of New York's Chinatown. Finally, people in Ah Maa's community, with the exception of a few entrepreneurs, come from a working-class background and survive in a mostly underground economy, some by living at the minimum-wage level.

The economic distinctions and lifestyles of the three groups are manifest in how they materialize their karaoke scenes. These people's karaoke webs of significance are spun and suspended in three different social spaces. (See Table 6.1 for a comparison across the three communities' karaoke dramaturgical webs that highlights some of these differences.) One can easily discern, for example, the extravagance embodied in the karaoke scenes in John's community as compared to the material simplicity of the karaoke scenes where people in Ah Maa's community mostly congregate. These webs do not intersect, for people do not readily cross between each other's karaoke spaces as a matter of course. People in these three interpretive communities do not have any genuine, sustained interclass social interaction.

In certain cases, some people in the New Jersey community were quite unwilling to be in any karaoke scenes that did not match their own. These

---

[1]Based on a literary analysis, Victoria Chen (1994) provided an insightful discussion on how certain second-generation Chinese Americans resolve some of the identity dilemmas they face.

TABLE 6.1
Comparison of Karaoke Scenes Across Three Communities

| | *Mrs. Chung's community* | *John's community* | *Ah Maa's community* |
|---|---|---|---|
| Social/economic class | Lower middle to middle class | Upper middle to upper class | Working to lower middle class |
| Occasions | Private parties, informal *yutkuk* practice, street parties on Chinese festival occasions | Private parties, monthly club meetings, lessons, annual or semiannual karaoke and dancing galas | Birthday parties, informal gatherings at ethnic karaoke clubs and restaurants |
| Episodes | Parties/rehearsals: solo and group singing among friends; festivals: solo or duet by *yamngok se* members and members from the audience, often juxtaposed with human and traffic noises in the street | Parties/rehearsals: solo singing, group singing only during practices; galas: well-dressed performers and (some) well-rehearsed and choreographed performances on stage, ballroom dancing a standard feature | Mostly solo performance but group singing is not unusual, dramatized interaction with little rehearsal |
| Settings | Privately owned spaces: houses and stores; public venues: streets | Expensive private homes (some with specially designed karaoke facilities), semipublic venues: fancy ballrooms at hotels and restaurants | Mostly public venues: local restaurants with karaoke equipment, small karaoke clubs open to the public |
| Props | Privately owned karaoke videocassette tape or laserdisc players, television monitors, large speaker system for street parties | Privately owned state-of-the-art karaoke technology, professional sound and lighting for galas, one club has own professional audiovisual equipment onstage | Mostly use moderate karaoke facility at restaurants and public clubs |
| Music | Mostly Cantonese opera songs, some Cantonese popular songs from Hong Kong | Mostly Mandarin songs, some Taiwanese and some English songs, a few Japanese-tinged songs (e.g., *enka*) | Mostly a mix of Mandarin and Cantonese songs, some Fukienese and some Taiwanese songs |
| Karaoke decorum | Courteous; tolerates interruptions or inattention at street parties; no organizational codes to follow; casual attire | Courteous; rules of engagement explicated organizationally, partisan applause likely at galas; casual to semiformal attire at private parties, semiformal to formal dress codes for galas | Courteous; no organizational codes to follow; casual attire |

people have better karaoke facilities at home than are found in typical Chinese restaurants. One such member saw it this way: "Those whose equipment is not as good as the clubs [that open to the public] may want to go to those clubs." According to this person's view, the karaoke facility that one has (or does not have) becomes a class symbol.

Asked if he had gone to karaoke clubs in Flushing, Queens, another affluent club member responded: "Flushing? No, it's too far away." But when I pressed further by suggesting that there were a few karaoke clubs in New Jersey that were open to the public, this man said:

> . . . I heard *the level of the people going to those clubs* [a pause here] . . . I don't know . . . . They smoke in the club, *wuyen changch'i* ["full of bad or filthy smoke and fume"]. Why are we going [there]? If we want to chat with our friends, it's comfortable to do so at home . . . . We haven't been to any of those clubs. (italics added)

Notice that this informant paused after his reference to "the level of the people going to those clubs." He quickly shifted to smoking and cigarette fumes as his reason for not going to "those clubs." But the aphorism *wuyen changch'i,* referring to bad smoke and smell at the sensory level, also is a value statement suggesting how a place is filled with social ill and filth. The aphorism might have been used connotatively at both the sensory and the social-valuative levels.

People in Ah Maa's and Mrs. Chung's communities are not entirely immune to this kind of social self-selectivity (or exclusivity), although I did observe on several occasions that people in the lower economic class seemed to be receptive to mixing with people from a higher economic class. At Ah Maa's first karaoke birthday, one of her friends brought her male employer and conspicuously introduced him with the words "He is a boss." People who overheard the introduction invariably turned their heads to the man. This introduction and the reaction it caused seemed to indicate a degree of class consciousness among people in this community, including the woman herself. But people at the party did not appear to reject the boss, although they initially maintained some distance from him. It was halfway into the night before he was able to blend in with a small group of guests active in singing karaoke. I cannot help but keep wondering how, without the woman as a guide, he might have otherwise fared with this crowd, many of whom survived on minimum wages from their own employers.

It is also important to note that, at the intracommunity level, members may have varying economic experiences. How individuals within a community engage karaoke certainly expresses their economic attainments and social status as members of that community. However, my comparative analysis of the three cases indicates that intragroup competition exists and that it is most pronounced in the affluent interpretive community in New Jersey. As analyzed in chapter 4, karaoke along with other signifying objects such as houses and music teachers establishes one's status within the community. This kind of intragroup comparison or competition does not seem to manifest itself in the other two interpretive communities.

## Expressions of Gendered Practice

As suggested in chapter 1, Rakow's (1988) gendered interpretation of technology enables us to conceptualize technology use as a social practice that reflects gender relations. Certain karaoke practices I observed in my ethnography indicate such gendered practices. For example, a woman club member once observed:

> Guys tend to like musical instruments more. If the husband doesn't want to buy [a karaoke machine], we wives just don't have it. I rarely see a guy buying [a karaoke machine] for his wife to sing. Maybe one or two. Guys like the wires, or things like that. We [women] tend to reject them. Our friends are mostly like that. When we have a gathering, the women usually get the tea and chat or something like that. When the guys are ready with the setup, we then go to sing. It's always the guy to initiate: "Let's sing karaoke."

Interestingly, this woman's experience echoes the experiences of Tim O'Sullivan's (1991) female informants, whose husbands tended to be the ones to decide on the purchase of family television sets (cited in Moores, 1993). Moores (1993) and Morley (1986) also found a tendency of male dominance in, respectively, the uses of early wireless and television remote control devices in domestic environments. In reference to O'Sullivan's finding, Moores (1993) observed: "No doubt, this can be explained by [men's] control over large items of household expenditure, but it is related, in addition, to the connections between masculinity and gadgetry" (p. 89).

Of course, one should be careful not to generalize the one woman's observation to the experience of all other female members of the community.[2] But the observation did come from within the community and

---

[2]It is important to note that the woman's statement does not refer to whether the women in her community are competent in handling technical gadgetry. I observed some of them capably operating relatively sophisticated electronic appliances at home. To a certain extent, I suspect that Ann Gray's (1986, 1992) observation of her subjects' "calculated ignorance" (cited in Moores, 1993, p. 94) can help us understand this aspect of the discussion. Gray discovered that some of the women she talked to did not want to learn how to operate their family's video recorder because that alleviated them from having an additional chore in the household. More research will have to be done to determine whether certain women in the New Jersey interpretive community maintain this calculated ignorance.

is purported to represent the experience of a large network maintained by the woman's family. Similarly, my field observations indicate that the men in the New Jersey community, as well as those in the other two communities, are more in control of the machine. For example, Mr. Hau and particularly Bill (Mrs. Chung's son) were always the ones to set up the karaoke *yutkuk* street parties. John had undisputed control of his karaoke ballroom. Calvin conceived and managed the entire technical set-up for a couple of galas after he became the president of his club. Carrying over the technical role in his club to other karaoke scenes, Ah Ting often played disc jockey at Ah Maa's birthday parties.

Other nontechnical activities also reveal the gendered nature of the three communities. The marriage requirement of private karaoke clubs in John's community essentially assumes, and is put in place to enforce, traditional family structure and, by implication, the heterosexual socio-moral order. The story of a karaoke-related affair that had been circulating among many people in this community also embodies such a worldview, which is also a male-dominated one. The married man in the narrative that was told to me repeatedly was the central character, while the other woman (also variously identified as simply "some woman" or "a woman") was portrayed on the sideline. The story never mentioned what might have happened to the man's wife during or after the alleged affair. The women in the story thus appear as passive, subordinate characters in a male-centered social and moral theater. Similarly, one may recall Calvin's Elvis act onstage, with the dancing girls playing the supporting roles.

In contrast, the action of Susan (in Ah Maa's community) in the late-night melodramatic excursion in the basement of the Southeast Asian restaurant expresses another kind of gendered power relations. The larger social world in which Susan lives is one of patriarchy. But although Susan was the romantic (or sexual) target of Denny and Ah Dong's flirtations, and thus their perceived or assumed subordinate figure, she was not truly a passive player in that karaoke episode. If she ever was the hunted, Susan certainly outmaneuvered her male pursuers. One may even suggest that Susan helped facilitate the episode so that she could enjoy the pleasure of the men's pursuit before discarding them. Susan's action was a symbolic gesture of her defiance of the passive, subordinate female gender role.

I am not suggesting that male dominance is absent from Susan's interpretive community, nor am I hinting that her compatriots enjoy symmetrical gender relations. After all, Ah Dong (and Denny) initially appeared to have assumed their lead and control. But Susan's action in that karaoke episode does reflect a degree of looseness in the social, interactional structure of her community's karaoke spaces. Unlike the karaoke webs in John's community (the galas, the music lessons, the monthly club meetings), which are themselves extensions of entrenched social institutions and norms (such as family, marriage, and corporate culture), those in Susan's community are, by the nature of the community itself, transitory. They are temporary, brief interactional structures where hegemonic social norms seem to be harder to enforce. The dramatic elements encoded in karaoke music and videos make the rules or patterns of human interaction in such a transitory space even more unstable and, to a certain extent, unpredictable. From Malaysia, Susan is out of reach of the social birthplace in which she is well connected and, from another perspective, constrained. As a global migrant, she can defy, to a certain extent, traditionally entrenched gendered roles while traveling in and through transitory social spaces both geosocially (Flushing, Queens) and dramaturgically (Ah Maa's karaoke birthday parties).

It is important to emphasize that, in the previous analysis, I do not make any valuative judgment of the moral worldviews of these people. Such evaluation and comparison is not the intent of this book. In this part of my discussion, I limit my analysis to how the divergent karaoke experiences reported in this book can be understood as expressions of certain gendered practices and social relations within each interpretive community.

In short, the divergent ethnic, social, economic, and gender frames of reference for people in the three interpretive communities—and the diverse karaoke experiences they engender—reflect the multiplicity and complexity of Chinese American culture. Although it is much easier for some people to view Chinese America as a homogeneous entity, such a view conceals much that is worth considering. At some level, it may also be easier and more convenient and comforting to view Chinese Americans (or Asian Americans as a whole) as a singular, model minority. However, such a view offers a picture of success, achievement, and happiness in the lives of some, and it shows little of how many others must confront hardship, neglect, and disappointment as they struggle in their everyday lives in the diaspora.

## THE INTERPLAY BETWEEN SOCIETY AND ITS TECHNOLOGY: THE KARAOKE EXPERIENCE

The karaoke experiences examined in this book express the relative ethnicity, social and economic class, and certain gendered practices and relations of people in the three interpretive communities. As we come to understand what people do in engaging karaoke for constructing, maintaining, or transforming social reality and meaning, we must also look at how their engagement with karaoke can at the same time redefine the nature of their social experience. The interaction between society and its technology is one of symbiosis; that is, they define and change one another as they interplay and evolve over time. From this perspective, the divergent karaoke experiences of the three interpretive communities illuminate a number of interesting issues. Although a lot can be said about the relationship between karaoke as a communication technology and society, the following section limits itself to three issues: namely, the nature of karaoke as a public form of social interaction, the literate character of karaoke music, and the indigenization of mass-mediated popular culture products.

## The Public Nature of Karaoke

The majority of the people in the three interpretive communities had no prior experience with amateur communal singing before encountering karaoke. As karaoke is adopted and incorporated into their everyday social existence, the practice also gradually (and to varying degrees) changes the nature of their social relations with others. Karaoke helps people in Mrs. Chung's community to extend their voices beyond the musical as well as social walls of their *yamngok se*. Many people in John's community stand the risk of being out of the loop if they do not have karaoke at home. Singing karaoke has become a defining communal experience for many people in Ah Maa's community. Across the three communities, singing in general and the singing of mass-mediated music in particular have certainly become part of the members' social and personal lives to an extent not previously encountered.[3]

What is equally important to point out is the public nature of karaoke interaction. Based on the experiences of the three interpretive communities, karaoke can be said to have helped bring social interaction outside people's homes and into public spaces. Changes in people's technological environment can redefine the nature of social interaction. The household faucet has been blamed for destroying people's communal life because they no longer have to go to the well, around which they can chat, exchange gossip, or otherwise socialize with their neighbors. Various electronic media, such as the telephone, the radio, and television, are also said to have turned social interaction in public spaces inward, to private settings (Aronson, 1986; Gumpert, 1987; McLuhan, 1976; Moores, 1993).

However, as the experiences of the three interpretive communities demonstrate, various kinds of social interaction are created and main-

---

[3]Changes of these kinds, in their various shapes and forms, are by no means confined to people in these three specific interpretive communities. Karaoke has become a fixture in a great many Asian American drinking and entertainment establishments. Singing at dinners or wedding banquets in Chinese American restaurants, for instance, is no longer an uncommon sight. The popularity and influence of karaoke as a social practice also seems to be widespread in many Chinese communities around the world (e.g., see "Karaoke is popular . . . ," 1992).

tained in public (and semipublic) places around karaoke. Put in another way, karaoke helps bring social interaction back to certain public spaces. If community is indeed "rooted in face-to-face dialogue between two or more people in the same place" (Gumpert, 1987, p. 177), karaoke encourages the formation of communities where participants converse, in the same physical space, through both everyday speech and musical dialogue. Mrs. Chung and her compatriots literally take part of their social life into the street. People in John's community move what used to be living-room-based social gatherings to such public spaces as catering halls, hotel ballrooms, and even high school auditoriums. People in Ah Maa's community congregate at restaurants and karaoke clubs open to the public where they constantly mingle with new and old acquaintances.

Of course, not all people or cultures react to this shift from the private to the public similarly. Marshall McLuhan (1976) once observed that "North Americans may well be the only people who go outside to be alone and inside to be social" (p. 46) and "it is not only in the movie and in the theatre that we seek privacy, but also at restaurants and in nightclubs" (p. 48). Karaoke as a practice is largely communal, hence demanding a degree of selflessness on the part of the participants. This may be one reason why many Americans still find it difficult to enter the stage area in karaoke bars to perform, that is, to be singled out, deprivatized, and to become social and communal in public spaces. Drew (1994) observed that, in managing their initial unease before and during their performance in karaoke bars, many Euro-Americans resort to getting half drunk or wearing dark glasses.

## The Literate Character of Karaoke Music

Karaoke also illuminates another interesting phenomenon. In karaoke, literacy has been pushed to the foreground in the consumption of a media form—music—that has traditionally been oral. Music and oral utterances have long been important means for human communication and expression and as mnemonics in societies where writing either does not exist or is not widespread. Of course, mass-mediated popular music, including karaoke music, is not exactly a primary or predominantly oral phenomenon. It is part of what Ong (1982) called a new or secondary orality that characterizes "present-day high-technology culture"; it is "sustained by telephone, radio, television, and other electronic devices that depend for their existence and functioning on writing and print" (p. 11). The narrative structure and orality of film and television, for example, is literacy-based. James M. Curtis (1978) spoke of the tension between orality and literacy in popular music: "Popular music comes from big business, and thus conforms to the structure of other types of Big Business in America. Although the musicians themselves have little to do with literacy, their lawyers and record companies emphatically have a great deal to do with literacy" (p. 163). Nonetheless, when people consume electronic mass media products, they normally watch (a television show, a movie, or a video) or listen (to music, the dialogue, or the radio). They normally do not read, unless subtitles are part of the product's visual components.

But reading texts (in the nonliterary critical sense) is by nature part of the karaoke consumption process. It is true that when people engage a karaoke video or audiotape, they also look at the pictures, listen to the music, or do both. But for those who have yet to memorize the song lyrics, reading the words running across the bottom of the video screen or in the songbook is an important part of the karaoke consumption and performative process. The majority of the people I document in this book (and in many other karaoke events not analyzed here) have to read the lyrics during their karaoke performance. Of course, those people who have rehearsed their songs before their formal performance, such as some club members in John's community or certain experienced Cantonese opera singers in Mrs. Chung's community, do not rely on the captions as much as those who have not practiced before performing in the stage area.

One of the implications of this literate bias[4] of karaoke is that it limits the participation of those who cannot read. Ah Maa's experience has been a most illuminating example. As much as she is eager to go to "the karaoke," Ah Maa's musical-performative engagement in karaoke scenes is very restricted. The fact that she does not read has confined her to only a few karaoke songs. Similar to the unaccompanied song her husband wrote for her, these few karaoke songs are memorized aurally and not in the image of written or printed words. This is the reason why, when I was singing with her, Ah Maa had to take aural cues by listening intently to me whenever she forgot the upcoming words.[5]

The rise of karaoke as a cultural practice should encourage intensified examination of the changing nature of our human, as well as media, ecology. In particular, although the paradigms of the media audience as receivers or readers are valuable conceptual and analytical tools, they are limited in explaining the role of the audience of interactive media forms. As we begin to understand the activity of karaoke consumers in hybridizing or indigenizing mass-mediated popular culture, we should also look at how people engage in similarly incomplete media. Such

---

[4]I use the word *bias* in this analysis in much the same way as Harold A. Innis (1951) did to explain the intrinsic spatial and temporal inclination of communication media.

[5]In recent follow-up conversations (in June 1995), Ah Maa told me she has already forgotten the song her husband wrote for her. The experience of Anne, the former cabaret singer, offers a similar example. Nonliterate in Chinese, she memorized songs in Chinese dialects such as Cantonese and Mandarin by listening to audio and videotapes imported from Hong Kong and Taiwan so that she could perform them at the nightclubs.

media are interactive and their semiotic resources, texts, or contents require the direct intervention of human users. How does one conceptualize the contents of such media as the telephone, electronic mail, virtual reality, the camcorder, desktop publishing, hypertext, and so forth, without considering human agency and creativity? What are the contents of such media forms if their consumers or audiences are not also seen as producers? What does presence of hybridized content tell us about their producers, their cultures, and the social conditions in which they live? In other words, it is essential to study people's creative and cultural involvement with these media forms as they set about constructing their personal as well as social lives.

More research is also needed before the nature of karaoke as a form of public social interaction can be better understood. As the earlier analysis suggests, people with different social frames of reference react to karaoke as a form of social interaction in divergent ways. How people in cultures where individualism and privacy are part of the group psyche manage their interaction with others in the context of karaoke (or other such public communal rituals) is an interesting cross- or intercultural analysis. Comparative analysis of whether and how karaoke is adopted (or rejected) in cultures around the world will offer insights to this important area of investigation. Such analysis of the cross-cultural adaptation of communication technologies is immensely valuable not only to scholars, but also to social policymakers—particularly when the pace of global migration quickens, the rate of international transfer of media forms increases, and the level of cultural and ethnic consciousness heightens.

At another level, the karaoke experience also brings our attention to the literacy-privileging feature of some of the latest developments in our electronic media environment. Karaoke is part of the latest evolution of electronic media, including the computer and teletext, of which literacy skills are an essential part. Various forms of virtual communities are formed in cyberspace (Jones, 1994; Strate, Jacobson, & Gibson, 1996), and interactions and their forms of discourse in these communities are sustained mostly by literacy. Those who are oral or nonliterate are mostly cut off from these kinds of encounters.

Of course, as the karaoke experiences analyzed in this book indicate, people's economic resources also determine the nature and extent of their access to these, or any other kinds of, communication technologies. In an age when the so-called information superhighway is becoming an integral part of the world's infrastructure for all sorts of interaction and transaction, and at a point in history when computer-based telecommunications are increasingly providing a forum for political participation (e.g., Abramson, Arterton, & Orren, 1988), the divide between the oral and the literate, as well as the divide between the technological haves and have-nots, may have an unsettling impact on our human, especially, democratic conditions.

## The Indigenization of Popular Culture Products

The experiences of the three interpretive communities support and return us to a central thesis of this book. The thesis argues that the media audiences of karaoke are not passive receivers of information, nor are they simply readers of media texts. Instead, they are active agents who, by employing a wide variety of social, material, and symbolic resources available in their environment, indigenize mass-mediated texts as part of their everyday production of social experiences and meanings.

Karaoke as a cultural practice is therefore inherently hybrid. Hybridization, Simon During (1993) suggested, is the process whereby "particular individuals and communities can actively create new meanings from signs and cultural products which come from afar" (p. 7). The hybrid nature of karaoke comes in part from the medium's deliberate semiotic incompleteness (music minus the lead vocal) in which codes are designed to incorporate direct human vocal and performative intervention. The hybridization that karaoke practices encapsulate is one of empowerment, in which human agency is at the foreground in the production of everyday cultures. The fact that most karaoke participants are simultaneously producer and audience also fosters dynamism in how people interact among themselves in the social contexts of karaoke.

In short, such a hybrid and empowering cultural practice as karaoke allows people a conspicuous degree of control in defining their own social worlds. Karaoke provides the social and symbolic structure for people to create, maintain, and transform social realities and meanings that are true and significant to them. Karaoke is by nature intensely indigenous because the unique blend of interpretive frame of reference, ethnicity, material expression, and gender arrangement that people bring to each and every performance defines the dramaturgical character, as well as the social and cultural experience, in the scene.

## ONE FINAL NOTE

The karaoke experiences of the three first-generation Chinese American interpretive communities tell the story of how people nurture various ways of life in environments not entirely familiar to them.[6] For people

---

[6]Part of the observation in this final section benefits from comments by William Starosta (Communication, Howard University) on some of the data as presented in a conference paper (Lum, 1995).

who have no prior experience in social singing, participating in a karaoke scene represents a new challenge, one that often invokes an enormous sense of uncertainty and anxiety. However, the frame of reference they bring with them—their past experiences, their aspirations—allows them not only to adopt to the new environments, but also redefine and shape them. In the process, they build communities, they construct identities in relation to others, and they establish a voice of their own. The same is true for those community members with prior social singing experiences; they too modify their backgrounds to contemporary circumstances, and in the process create new communication forms and social networks.

To a certain extent, these people's karaoke experiences symbolize part of the American immigrant experience. For many new immigrants in all ages, coming to the United States is an experience that is as uncertain and anxiety-provoking as it is full of possibilities and excitement. They have to adjust to many explicit as well as implicit rules pre-existing in the social environment that they are new participants of. They have to confront the likelihood of humiliation, defeat, or even abuse. But as they adapt to and become a part of the new environment, they also change some of the rules that once restricted them. Their determination, ingenuity, and hard work allow them to build communities, to construct distinct identities, and to establish communications that were once unknown or ignored. This is the American immigrant spirit. The United States is indeed a nation of immigrants, with people from all shores and every corner of the world, and the immigrant experience is an integral part of the American experience. From this perspective, we may begin to regard the American experience as an orchestra of cultures, one where each culture plays a distinct note in the chorus of the collective social existence and where, as in karaoke scenes, people's individual voices can be found and heard.

# Appendix

## Notes on Methodology

This book is part of an ongoing research program on the cultural history of Chinese-language media in the United States (see Lum, 1991, 1994a, 1996). Field research for this book was begun in the summer of 1993 and completed in early 1995. Follow-up communication with key informants continued until June 1995. I chose to focus my analysis on first-generation immigrants because their experience of being uprooted gives us a unique angle to look at the role of the media in people's adaptation from one social and cultural space to another.

In the beginning of my field research, I did not perceive or conceive of any of my informants as part of an interpretive community, although it was amply clear to me at the time that they tended to cluster with people from a similar social, economic, and ethnic background. The notion of three distinct interpretive strategies came to the foreground about 6 to 10 months after beginning fieldwork when I was reviewing some of my findings in consultation with my editors.

Original data for this book came from participant observation of select karaoke scenes, where people from the three interpretive communities performed and congregated, and from in-depth interviews of a selection of people who participated in these scenes. After several months of informal conversation and more systematic observation of people's interaction at numerous karaoke scenes, an average of two dozen informants from each community was selected for private interviewing. These people were selected because, in my judgment, their demographic profiles and ways of engaging karaoke as a cultural practice were emerging in preliminary analysis as typical of people in their respective communities. Videotapes made at various karaoke scenes, either by me or supplied by my informants, have supplemented participant observations and informant testimonies.

I came to know the people described in this book mostly through informal channels. Personal acquaintances introduced me to these people at various karaoke scenes, and the network of informants gradually snowballed over a 2-year period, with one exception. I established my initial contact with Mrs. Chung after reading and responding to her announcement in a Chinese newspaper for her karaoke street party in 1993.

The fact that I am a first-generation Chinese American immigrant and speak native Cantonese and fluent Mandarin and English helped me gain entry into these several groups of people. In general, the people in the three communities have been friendly and receptive to my presence. Otherwise, they would not have shared with me an important part of their social, cultural, and, to a certain extent, their personal life experiences; and I would not have had adequate data with which to write this book.

Comparatively, my Hong Kong background made it easier for me to establish relations with people in Mrs. Chung's community. I did not stand out among them because, among other things, we shared stories from Hong Kong that only locals would understand and appreciate. However, my Hong Kong background did not particularly help me with the other two communities, even though it did not do any apparent damage either. Fortunately, my initial entry into the affluent New Jersey group was aided by someone respected by my first informants there. Similarly, my contact for Ah Maa's group in Flushing, Queens, was well-connected in the community.

My identity as a college professor has been a mixed blessing to my fieldwork. Professors and scholars belong to a relatively respected and privileged class in certain Chinese communities. Although this part of my identity seemed to help me win some acceptance from my informants in the three communities, it also created certain inconveniences. On several occasions, when my professorial identity was revealed in introduction, it tended to take extra effort and time on my part to divert people's attention from my work to what they were supposed to be doing at the scene. Fortunately, this was not a frequent occurrence and when the music was playing, any attention that people might have placed on me and my work tended to be redirected. Moreover, this kind of inconvenience usually occurred at very small gatherings with about 15 or fewer participants. My presence at larger scenes apparently was not as conspicuous.

To honor my informants' request for and right to confidentiality, I have altered their names in this report. To preserve the voice inherent in their names, I have substituted an Anglicized name with another Anglicized name and a Chinese name with another Chinese name. Chinese names or words are transliterated according to their specific regional roots or pronunciation. Because no single system can effectively Romanize the extremely diverse Chinese dialects, unless otherwise indicated, Cantonese words are romanized in the Yale system (Huang & Kok, 1960; see also Yung, 1989, pp. 158–161, for a concise discussion of the application of the Yale system) and words originally pronounced in Mandarin are romanized in the Thomas Wade system (Liang, 1972). Cantonese is the predominant dialect in chapters 3 and 5 and Mandarin in chapter 4.

To ensure as accurate an understanding of the findings as possible, I triangulated the people's interpretations of their own individual experience, their interpretations of the experience of others in their respective communities, and my observation of their behavior in its natural environment, and framed all this against the larger social and cultural experience of Chinese American immigrants. However, because any ethnographic writing is necessarily a construction of a construction, that is, the writer's rendering of how the natives view what happens in their life world (Geertz, 1973), then it must be acknowledged that the karaoke experiences of the people I present in this book are, indeed, and with no pretense, my interpretation.

# References

Abramson, J. B., Arterton, F., & Orren, G. R. (1988). *The electronic commonwealth: The impact of new media technologies on democratic politics.* New York: Basic Books.

Adorno, T., & Horkheimer, M. (1977). The culture industry (abridged). In J. Curran, M. Gurevitch, & J. Woollacott (Eds.), *Mass communication and society* (pp. 349–383). London: Edward Arnold.

Armstrong, L. (1992, June 8). What's that noise in aisle 5? *Business Week,* p. 38.

Aronson, S. H. (1986). The sociology of the telephone. In G. Gumpert & R. Cathcart (Eds.), *Inter/media: Interpersonal communication in a media world* (3rd ed., pp. 300–310). New York: Oxford University Press.

Ban, S. (1991, April). Everyone's a star. *Look Japan,* pp. 40-42.

Bauman, R., & Sherzer, J. (Eds.). (1989). *Explorations in the ethnography of speaking* (2nd ed.). Cambridge, England: Cambridge University Press.

Bineham, J. L. (1988). A historical account of the hypodermic model in mass communication. *Communication Monographs, 55*(3), 230–246.

Bunge, F. M. (Ed.). (1984). *Malaysia: A country study.* Washington, DC: The American University.

Carey, J. W. (1988). *Communication as culture.* Boston: Unwin Hyman.

Carey, J. W. (1995). Abolishing the old spirit world. *Critical Studies in Mass Communication, 12*(1), 82–89.

Chan, S. Y. (1991). *Improvisation in a ritual context: The music of Cantonese opera.* Hong Kong: The Chinese University Press.

Chan, S. (Ed.). (1991). *Entry denied: Exclusion and the Chinese community in America, 1882–1943.* Philadelphia: Temple University Press.

Chang, T.-K. (1983). *The Chinese press in U. S.: A linkage to the past.* Paper presented to Association for Education in Journalism and Mass Communication Annual Convention, Corvallis, OR.

Chang, Y. S. (1990, December 8). Chinese-language television in Northern California: Entering a period of the Warring States [in Chinese]. *China Times Weekly,* American edition, pp. 74–75.

Chen, H.-s. (1992). *Chinatown no more: Taiwan immigrants in contemporary New York.* Ithaca, NY: Cornell University Press.

Chen, H.-s. (1993). Chinese in Chinatown and Flushing [ref. A/AC RE-901101]. Flushing, NY: Asian/American Center, Queens College.

Chen, V. (1994). (De)hyphenated identity: The double voice in *The woman warrior.* In A. Gonzalez, M. Houston, & V. Chen (Eds.), *Our voices: Essays in culture, ethnicity, and communication* (pp. 3–11). Los Angeles: Roxbury.

Cheng, H. Y. (1990, December 8). Uncovering the history of New York's Chinese-language television [in Chinese]. *China Times Weekly,* American edition, pp. 73–74.

Cloud, D. L. (1992). The limits of interpretations: Ambivalence and the stereotype in "Spenser: For Hire." *Critical Studies in Mass Communication, 9*(4), 311–324.

Cooley, C. H. (1909). *Social organization: A study of the larger mind.* New York: Scribner's.

Curtis, J. M. (1978). *Culture as polyphony: An essay on the nature of paradigms.* Columbia: University of Missouri Press.

De Mente, B. (1989). *Everything Japanese.* Lincolnwood, IL: NTC Publishing Group.

Deutsch, C. H. (1994, October 2). A Chinatown with a polyglot accent. *The New York Times,* Section 9, pp. 1, 13.

Dewey, J. (1916). *Democracy and education.* New York: Macmillan.

Doyle, J., & Khandelwal, M. (1993). Asians and Pacific Islanders enumerated in the 1990 census [ref. A/AC RE-9311011]. Flushing, NY: Asian/American Center, Queens College.

Drew, R. S. (1994). *Where the people are the real stars: An ethnography of karaoke bars in Philadelphia.* Unpublished doctoral dissertation, University of Pennsylvania, Philadelphia.

During, S. (1993). Introduction. In S. During (Ed.), *The cultural studies reader.* London: Routledge.

Eisenstein, E. L. (1979). *The printing press as an agent of change.* New York: Cambridge University Press.

Eisenstein, E. L. (1983). *The printing revolution in early modern Europe.* New York: Cambridge University Press.

Enzensberger, H. M. (1974). *The consciousness industry.* New York: Seabury Press.

Ewen, S. (1976). *Captains of consciousness.* New York: McGraw-Hill.

Feiler, B. S. (1991). *Learning to bow: Inside the heart of Japan.* New York: Ticknor & Fields.

Fish, S. (1980). *Is there a text in this class?* Cambridge, MA: Harvard University Press.

Fiske, J. (1987). *Television culture.* New York: Methuen.

Fleck, L. (1979). *Genesis and development of a scientific fact.* Chicago: The University of Chicago Press.

Fornäs, J. (1994). Karaoke: Subjectivity, play and interactive media. *The Nordicom Review of Nordic Research on Media & Communication, 1,* 87–103.

Gandy, O. H., Jr. (Ed.). (1995). Colloquy. *Critical Studies in Mass Communication, 12*(1), 60–100.

Garnham, N. (1990). *Capitalism and communication: Global culture and economics of information.* London: Sage.

Geertz, C. (1973). *The interpretation of cultures.* New York: Basic Books.

Gencarelli, T. F. (1993). *Reading "heavy metal" music: An interpretive communities approach to popular music as communication.* Unpublished doctoral dissertation, New York University.

Gerbner, G. (Ed.). (1983). Ferment in the field [Special issue]. *Journal of Communication, 33*(3).

Goffman, E. (1959). *The presentation of self in everyday life.* New York: Doubleday Anchor.

Goffman, E. (1983). The interaction order. *American Sociological Review, 48,* 1–17.

Gray, A. (1986). *Video recorders in the home: Women's work and boys' toys.* Paper presented to the Second International Television Studies Conference, London.

Gray, A. (1992). *Video playtime: The gendering of a leisure technology.* London: Routledge.

Gumpert, G. (1987). *Talking tombstones & other tales of the media age.* New York: Oxford University Press.

Hall, S. (1980). Encoding/decoding. In S. Hall, D. Hobson, A. Lowe, & P. Willis (Eds.), *Culture, media, language* (pp. 128–138). London: Hutchinson.

Havelock, E. A. (1976). *Origins of western literacy.* Canada: The Ontario Institute for Studies in Education.

Heath, S. (1977–1978). Notes on suture. *Screen, 18*(4), 48–76.

Hebdige, D. (1979). *Subculture: The meaning of style.* London: Methuen.

Hing, B. O. (1993). *Making and remaking Asian America through immigration policy, 1850–1990.* Stanford, CA: Stanford University Press.

Hu, J. C. (1994). *Festivals: Traditional Chinese festivals* (6th ed.). Taipei, Taiwan: Kwang Kwa.

Hu, W. C. (1990). *The Chinese Mid-Autumn festival: Foods & folklore.* Ann Arbor, MI: Ars Ceramica.

Huang, P. P., & Kok, G. P. (1960). *Speak Cantonese.* New Haven, CT: Yale University, Institute of Far Eastern Studies.

Hymes, D. (1975). Breakthrough into performance. In D. Ben-amos & K. Goldstein (Eds.), *Folklore: Performance and communication* (pp. 11–74). The Hague: Mouton.

Innis, H. A. (1951). *The bias of communication.* Toronto, Canada: The University of Toronto Press.

Isajiw, W. W. (1974). Definitions of ethnicity. *Ethnicity, 1,* 111–124.

Jensen, K. B. (1990). Television futures: A social action methodology for studying interpretive communities. *Critical Studies of Mass Communication, 7*(2), 129–146.

Jensen, K. B. (1993). The past in the future: Problems and potentials of historical reception studies. *Journal of Communication, 43*(4), 20–28.

Jones, S. G. (Ed.). (1994). *Cybersociety: Computer-mediated communication and community.* Thousand Oaks, CA: Sage.

Karaoke. (1993, July 23). Special feature on night life [in Chinese]. *Next Magazine,* pp. 48–55.

Karaoke is popular in Chinese communities around the world [in Chinese]. (1992, December 27). *China Times Weekly,* American edition, pp. 8–13.

Kuhn, T. S. (1970). *The structure of scientific revolutions* (2nd ed.). Chicago: The University of Chicago Press.

Kwok, J. C. (1985). *Changes of Chinatown: Historical anecdotes of New York's Chinatown* [in Chinese]. Hong Kong: Po I Publishing.

Kwong, P. (1987). *The new Chinatown.* New York: Noonday Press.

Lee, R. H. (1960). *The Chinese in the United States of America.* Hong Kong: Hong Kong University Press.

Leeds-Hurwitz, W. (1993). *Semiotics and communication—Signs, codes, cultures.* Hillsdale, NJ: Lawrence Erlbaum Associates.

Leeds-Hurwitz, W., Sigman, S. J., & Sullivan, S. J. (1995). Social communication theory: Communication structures and performed invocations, a revision of Scheflen's notion of programs. In S. Sigman (Ed.), *The consequentiality of communication* (pp. 163–204). Hillsdale, NJ: Lawrence Erlbaum Associates.

Levy, M. R. (Ed.). (1993). The future of the field II [Special issue]. *Journal of Communication, 43*(4).

Li, C. H. (1992, December 27). The sound of karaoke is heard everywhere: Taipei [in Chinese]. *China Times Weekly,* American edition, pp. 14–15.

Li, L. (1993, May). Taiwan's culture of carousing. *Sinorama,* pp. 76–83.

Liang, S.-c. (Ed.). (1972). Wade Romanization index. In *A new practical Chinese-English dictionary* (pp. 1315–1353). Taipei, Taiwan: Far East Book.

Lii, J. H. (1995, January 8). Dateline: Chinatown. Four Chinese dailies see the news from different angles. *The New York Times,* p. 9.

Lin, F, & Lu, C. (1992, December 27). The sound of karaoke is heard everywhere: Hong Kong [in Chinese]. *China Times Weekly,* American edition, p. 15.

Lin, K. (1990, December 8). Los Angeles: A heated market for Chinese-language television [in Chinese]. *China Times Weekly,* American edition, pp. 68–71.

Livingstone, S. M. (1993). The rise and fall of audience research: An old story with a new ending. *Journal of Communication, 43*(4), 5–12.

Lu, C. (1992, December 27). The sound of karaoke is heard everywhere: Guangzhou [in Chinese]. *China Times Weekly,* American edition, p. 16.

Lum, C. M. K. (1991). Communication and cultural insularity: The Chinese immigrant experience. *Critical Studies in Mass Communication, 8*(1), 91–101.

Lum, C. M. K. (1994a). Regionalism and communication: Exploring Chinese immigrant perspectives. In A. Gonzalez, M. Houston, & V. Chen (Eds.), *Our voices: Essays in culture, ethnicity, and communication* (pp. 146–151). Los Angeles: Roxbury.

Lum, C. M. K. (1994b, April). *The revolt of the audience: Empowerment and the role of the audience/performer in karaoke.* Paper presented to the 85th annual convention of the Eastern Communication Association, Washington, DC.

Lum, C. M. K. (1995, April). *Karaoke and the re/construction of culture and ethnicity.* Paper (and video excerpts) presented at the 86th Eastern Communication Association Conference, Pittsburgh, PA.

Lum, C. M. K. (1996). Chinese cable television: Social activism, community service and non-profit media in New York's Chinatown. In G. Gumpert & S. Drucker (Eds.), *Communication and immigration.* Cresskill, NJ: Hampton Press.

Ma, R. (1994, April). *Ethos derived from karaoke performance in Taiwan.* Paper presented at the 85th Eastern Communication Association Conference, Washington, DC.

MacCabe, C. (1974). Realism and the cinema: Notes on some Brechtian theses. *Screen, 15*(2), 7–27.

Malinowski, B. (1956). The problem of meaning in primitive languages. In C. K. Ogden & I. A. Richards (Eds.), *The meaning of meaning* (pp. 296–336). New York: Harcourt Brace.

Marcuse, H. (1964). *One dimensional man.* Boston: Beacon Press.

Mark, D. M. L., & Chih, G. (1982). *A place called Chinese America.* Dubuque, IA: Kendall/Hunt.

McLuhan, M. (1976). Inside on the outside, or the spaced-out American. *Journal of Communication, 26*(4), 46–53.

Min, P. G. (1994). *Asian Americans: Contemporary trends and issues.* Thousand Oaks, CA: Sage.

Ming, H. (1992, December 27). The sound of karaoke is heard everywhere: Beijing [in Chinese]. *China Times Weekly,* American edition, p. 17.

Mitsui, T. (1991, July). *Karaoke: How the combination of technology and music evolved?* Paper presented at the 6th International Conference on Popular Music Studies, Berlin, Germany.

Moores, S. (1993). *Interpreting audiences: The ethnography of media consumption.* London: Sage.

Morley, D. (1980). *The "Nationwide" audience: Structure and decoding.* London: British Film Institute.

Morley, D. (1986). *Family television: Cultural power and domestic leisure.* London: Comedia.

Morley, D. (1993). Active audience theory: Pendulums and pitfalls. *Journal of Communication, 43*(4), 13–19.

Nunziata, S. (1990, January 6). U.S. karaoke outfit plans to enter American market. *Billboard,* pp. 12, 88.

Ogawa, H. (1990, October). The karaoke way. *Pacific Friend,* p. 32.

Ogawa, H. (1993a, July). *Karaoke in Japan: A sociological overview.* Paper presented at the 8th International Conference on Popular Music Studies, Stockton, CA.

Ogawa, H. (1993b, May). Unstoppable karaoke. *Pacific Friend,* pp. 17–21.

Ong, W. J. (1982). *Orality and literacy.* New York: Methuen.

O'Sullivan, T. (1991). Television memories and cultures of viewing, 1950–65. In J. Corner (Ed.), *Popular television in Britain: Studies in cultural history* (pp. 159–81). London: British Film Institute.

Pan, L. (1990). *Sons of the yellow emperor: A history of the Chinese Diaspora.* Boston: Little, Brown.

Parenti, M. (1986). *Inventing reality.* New York: St. Martin's Press.

Park, R. (1920). Foreign language press and social progress. *Proceedings of the National Conference of Social Work,* 493–500.

Park, R. (1922). *The immigrant press and its control.* New York: Harper & Brothers.

Park, R. (1925). Immigrant community and immigrant press. *American Review, 3,* 143–152.

Postman, N. (1985). *Amusing ourselves to death.* New York: Viking.

Radway, J. (1984). *Reading the romance: Women, patriarchy, and popular literature* (With a new introduction). Chapel Hill: University of North Carolina Press.

Rakow, L. F. (1988). Gendered technology, gendered practice. *Critical Studies in Mass Communication, 5*(1), 57–70.

Riddle, R. (1978). Music clubs and ensembles in San Francisco's Chinese community. In B. Nettl (Ed.), *Eight urban musical cultures: Tradition and change* (pp. 223–259). Urbana: University of Illinois Press.

Riddle, R. (1983). *Flying dragons, flowing streams—Music in the life of San Francisco's Chinese.* Westport, CT: Greenwood.

Schaefer, R. T. (1979). *Racial and ethnic groups.* Boston: Little, Brown.

Scheflen, A. E. (1964). The significance of posture in communication systems. *Psychiatry, 27,* 316–331.

Scheflen, A. E. (1965). *Systems in human communication.* Paper presented at the meeting of the American Association for the Advancement of Science, Berkeley, CA.

Scheflen, A. E. (1979). On communication processes. In A. Wolfgang (Ed.), *Nonverbal behavior: Applications and cultural implications* (pp. 1–16). New York: Academic Press.

Schiller, H. I. (1973). *The mind managers.* Boston: Beacon Press.

Schiller, H. I. (1989). *Culture Inc.: The corporate takeover of public expression.* New York: Oxford University Press.

Shelley, R. (1993). *Culture shock! Japan.* Portland, OR: Times Editions Pte Ltd./Graphic Arts Center Publishing.

Sloop, J. M. (1994). "Apology made to whoever pleases": Cultural discipline and the grounds of interpretation. *Communication Quarterly, 42*(4), 345–362.

Sontag, D. (1993, September 2). Study sees illegal aliens in new light. *The New York Times,* pp. B1, B8.

Sproule, J. M. (1989). Progressive propaganda critics and the magic bullet myth. *Critical Studies in Mass Communication, 6*(3), 225–246.

Steiner, L. (1988). Oppositional decoding as an act of resistance. *Critical Studies in Mass Communication, 5*(1), 1–15.

Strate, L., Jacobson, R., & Gibson, S. B. (Eds.). (1996). *Communication and cyberspace.* Cresskill, NJ: Hampton Press.

Straubhaar, J., & LaRose, R. (1996). *Communication media in the information society.* Belmont, CA: Wadsworth.

Takaki, R. (1989). *Strangers from another shore.* Boston: Little, Brown.

Tanaka, Y. (Ed.). (1990). *Japan as it is: A bilingual guide* (Rev. ed.). Tokyo: Gakken.

Thomas, S. (Ed.). (1990). Reading recent revisionism. *Critical Studies in Mass Communication, 8*(4).

Thomas, S. (Ed.). (1991). Media interpretation. *Critical Studies in Mass Communication, 7*(2).

U.S. Bureau of the Census. (1993). *Statistical abstract of the United States* (113th ed.). Washington, DC: U.S. Government Printing Office.

Wei, H.-c. (1992, April). Cramming for karaoke. *Sinorama,* pp. 38–41.

Weinstein, E. (1969). The development of interpersonal competence. In D. A. Goslin (Ed.), *Handbook of socialization theory and research* (pp. 753–775). Chicago: Rand McNally.

White, L., Jr. (1962). *Medieval technology and social change.* New York: Oxford University Press.

White, M. (1993). *The material child: Coming of age in Japan and America.* New York: The Free Press.

Williams, R. (1965). *The long revolution.* New York: Penguin.

Wolfe, A. S. (1992). Who's gotta have it?: The ownership of meaning and mass media texts. *Critical Studies in Mass Communication, 9*(3), 261–276.

Wong, B. (1985). Family, kinship, and ethnic identity of the Chinese in New York City, with comparative remarks on the Chinese in Lima, Peru and Manila, Philippines. *Journal of Comparative Family Studies, 16*(2), 231–254.

Wong, C.-H. (1990). *Forty years of Cantonese popular songs* [in Chinese]. Hong Kong: Joint Publishing Company.

Wong, D. (1994). I want the microphone: Mass mediation and agency in Asian American popular music. *The Drama Review, 38*(2), 152–167.

Wu, E. (1993, July). The KTV craze. *Free China Review,* p. 9.

Yung, B. (1989). *Cantonese opera: Performance as creative process.* Cambridge, England: Cambridge University Press.

Zhang, W.-h. A. (1994). *The musical activities of the Chinese American communities in the San Francisco Bay Area: A social and cultural study.* Unpublished doctoral dissertation, University of California, Berkeley.

Zheng, S. (1993). *Immigrant music and transnational discourse: Chinese American music culture in New York City.* Unpublished doctoral dissertation, Wesleyan University, Middletown, CT.

Zhou, M. (1992). *Chinatown: The socioeconomic potential of an urban enclave.* Philadelphia: Temple University Press.

Zimmerman, K. (1991, August 5). Can karaoke carry U. S. tune? *Variety,* pp. 1, 108.

# Author Index

# Subject Index

scene (defined), 11
singing lessons, 69–70
and social amateur singing, 9
and social membership, 9
social origins of, 8–10
as status symbol, 54–75
as a technology for communication,
4–6, 9

**L**

Literacy
and Cantonese opera, 40
and karaoke, 109–112
-privileging features of certain modern
media, 111
*Lou hwakiu* ("old overseas Chinese"),
24–26, *see also* Chinatown and
"bachelor society"

**M**

Magic bullet theory, 14–15
Media audience
as producer (of indigenized culture),
18–19
as reader (of media texts), 14–17
Melodrama (in karaoke terms), 94–96
Mid–Autumn Festival, 34–35, 49–52

**O**

Oppositional decoding, 16
Orchestra of cultures, 113, *see also* Immigrant experience as American
experience

**P**

Paradigm, 20–21, *see also* Thought style
Performance (defined), 18–19
Political economy, 15
Popular music, *see also* Karaoke mu-
sic/songs
the indigenization of, 112
Printing press, 4–5
Private karaoke clubs, 58–61
corporate managerial mannerism ex-
pressed in, 61
Programs (of behavior), 11, 52
Public space, *see* Karaoke and public
space

**R**

Racial hostility, 24

Regionalism, 25, 101–102
and the Chinese identity, 25
Research methods,
ethnography, 17
notes on (used in this book), 114–116
participant observation, 114, *see also*
Identity of author and its implications in research
videotaping, 114
Roles of karaoke participants, 12–13
Romanization (of Chinese words), 115–116

**S**

"Screen" theory, 15, *see also* Media audi-
ence as reader
Semiotics, 15
Silent participation in karaoke scenes,
88–92
Social reality, 7, 14, 21–22, 30, 92, 107,
*see also* Melodrama
Sociomoral order, 61–65
Stage area vs. audience area, 11–12
Status symbol (karaoke teacher as a),
70–72, *see also* Class
Styles, 14, 19

**T**

Technology
adaptation of, 3–6
for communication defined, 4–6
and the democratic conditions, 111–112
gendered use of, 5
vs. medium, 6
and social change in Medieval Europe,
5–6
unforeseen consequences or possibilities of, 6, 98
of writing, 4
Television
Chinese-language, *see also* Chinese-
language media
remote control device, 5
Theoretical assumptions, 3
Thought style, 20–21

**V**

Voice
alternative (voices) in society, 15–16
in informants' names, 115
media and the construction of, 23, 26,
28, 88
social and cultural, 52, 88, 97–99,
112–113